# Praise for *Ordinary Time*

"Oh, wow, do I love this book! Annie B. Jones has written something so thoughtful and beautifully earnest in the best way. *Ordinary Time* wears its earnestness as a well-deserved badge of honor; it's an inspiration to all of us to be true to ourselves, true to what we love, and true to the quiet voice within us. What a gift! This book is an ode to loving where you are, loving the small places, the cracks where the light gets in, the deceptively simple, the small yet impossibly intricate. *Ordinary Time* is a book for anyone who has wondered about their place in the world. I can't wait to return to it again and again."

—R. Eric Thomas, bestselling author of *Here for It*

"In *Ordinary Time*, Annie B. Jones turns mundanity into meaning—giving her readers a beautifully told and deeply considered account of the everyday choices that pile up to become a life. It reads like a soothing conversation with a trustworthy friend."

—Mary Laura Philpott, author of
*I Miss You When I Blink* and *Bomb Shelter*

"Thoughtful childhood nostalgia and stories that find the magic in the mundane will be especially touching for millennials."

—Erin Napier, bestselling author of *Heirloom Rooms* and coauthor of *Make Something Good Today*

"Annie B. Jones speaks right to this childhood bookworm who once thought the key to being interesting was seeking an adventurous life, but who now craves the beauty of an ordinary day. In friendship, vocation, faith, and home, readers of *Ordinary Time* will find relief and relatability in her words about the power of staying."

—Laura Tremaine, author of *The Life Council* and *Share Your Stuff. I'll Go First.*

"You've been waiting for this book; you just didn't know it. But believe me, you will."

—Sean Dietrich, columnist, podcaster, and author of *Kinfolk* and *You Are My Sunshine*

"I thought I was coming for the book talk, and it didn't disappoint. But the stories that really captured my imagination and have lived in my head since I first read them are about entirely different things: line dancing in a high school gym, the virtue of affability, a house with a pool. *Ordinary Time* feels like a long conversation with a good friend about the things in life that matter most, the kind of talk that leaves you feeling both grounded and inspired. Until now, most of us have known Annie B. Jones as a reader and bookstore owner. Now I'm excited for the world to get to know her as a writer as well."

—Anne Bogel, host of *What Should I Read Next*
and author of *I'd Rather Be Reading*

"I am a leaver, not a stayer, moving from the Deep South to New York as soon as I could, and I still saw so much of myself in this book. Annie's stories connect us all as daughters, sisters, friends, and obsessive lovers of *Fleabag*."

—Elizabeth Passarella, author of *Good Apple*
and *It Was an Ugly Couch Anyway*

"Annie writes a love letter to everyone who's ever wondered if they made the right choice to stay, to stick around, to continue on. I absolutely adored the tender way she carries her stories of remaining, and how she shares them to remind us of our long obedience in the same direction."

—Erin Hicks Moon, author of *I've Got Questions*
and host of the *Faith Adjacent* podcast

"What a privilege it is to go along with Annie B. Jones on her journey of staying put. Earnest, graceful, and beautifully written, this book is an exquisite reflection on the art of finding enchantment in ordinary time. This is one to treasure and come back to again and again."

—Annabel Monaghan, author of *Summer Romance*
and *Nora Goes Off Script*

"Annie B. Jones has a gift for putting complicated feelings into words—I lost count of the times I thought, 'me too!' as I read these pages. *Ordinary Time* is a book that will help you appreciate the satisfaction of quiet days, find joy even in complicated community, and see the beauty of ending up in a life you never expected. Annie has written a lovely book about the pain of good-byes and the surprises that can happen when you choose to stay put."

—Kerry Winfrey, author of *Waiting for Tom Hanks*
and *Very Sincerely Yours*

# Ordinary Time

# Ordinary Time

## Lessons Learned While Staying Put

# Annie B. Jones

**HARPERONE**

*An Imprint of* HarperCollins*Publishers*

HarperCollins books may be purchased for educational, business, or sales promotional use. For information, please email the Special Markets Department at SPsales@harpercollins.com.

FIRST EDITION

*Designed by Yvonne Chan*

Library of Congress Cataloging-in-Publication Data has been applied for.

ISBN 978-0-06-341127-2

25 26 27 28 29 LBC 5 4 3 2 1

*For*

*Carl and Annie Ruth*

*Charles and Linda*

*What a privilege to be your granddaughter.*

*Thank you for showing me how to stay.*

*Still, there are times I am bewildered by each mile I have traveled, each meal I have eaten, each person I have known, each room in which I have slept. As ordinary as it all appears, there are times when it is beyond my imagination.*

—Jhumpa Lahiri, *Interpreter of Maladies*

*I just hate the idea that a person has to live in a big city in order to write. I hate that.*

—Hannah Pittard, *We Are Too Many*

# CONTENTS

# CONTENTS

## Part IV: Staying Grounded

## Part V: Staying You

# Foreword

I met Annie B. Jones in the summer of 2019 when I cohosted a group of writers and small business owners on a trip to London. My role on the trip was to hold space for conversation, to ask good questions, and to hopefully foster connection and support. On the day they arrived in Brenchley, the quiet village in Kent where we would be staying, we planned to take a walk to acclimate their minds and bodies to the time change, a feeble attempt to stave off jetlag.

I have a distinct memory of catching a distant glimpse of Annie across the grounds of All Saints Church, a tiny parish near the guesthouse. She walked slowly through the gravestones in the cemetery surrounding the church, her tan travel pants blending into the landscape. And though she had never been there before, she somehow looked at home among it all, quiet as she walked, thoughtful, and at peace. Here was a woman who seemed content in her own skin, easily pleased by simple things, grateful to be wherever she is. Years later, when she first told me that she would like very much to write about staying put and to craft a collection of stories about being a person who is rooted in a world that is rootless, nothing made more sense. I felt about her not-yet-to-be book the way I felt about her: *I wanted more.*

We are, all of us, stayers and leavers. I have been loyal to one man and one town and one perfect collection of paint colors for twenty-five years (Alabaster White, Oyster Bay, Tricorn Black, and Sea Salt forever). I have also said difficult goodbyes to friends, communities, jobs, and a handful of tired ideologies. I'm sure you've done some version of the same. To be human is to know what it feels like to sit all the way down for the long haul, to stand all the way up and leave rooms that no longer fit, and to carry the sorrows and celebrations that may accompany both.

This is a book about a human experience we all share but may rarely have occasion to talk about: the things you let go and the things you hold on to when you are the one who stays. Earnest and endearing, these stories are small ones, and I don't mean they are *unimportant* (why do we so often conflate those two words?). Rather they are treasure-worthy, ones you'll be delighted to find and compelled to hold.

The plot is a gentle one yet somehow, impossibly, I found myself wanting to watch a movie about this invitational kind of life, one that doesn't demand attention but *lives* in the kind of way I think we all want to when we grow tired of striving after sparkly things, of trying to prove ourselves, and of nursing that nagging feeling that something is missing. Hers is a life of meaningful presence and in sharing it, Annie invites us to reflect on our own.

If you could somehow combine the voices of Wendell Berry and Norah Ephron, you might get something that looks a lot like *Ordinary Time*. Welcome to a story of small arrows pointing to simple places where you might find God: while being the older sister to one brother, in owning a bookshop in a small town in South Georgia, or on the front porch of your childhood home. Welcome to a story of namesake and legacy, of choosing to stay and of saying goodbye. Welcome to a story of love and loss, hope and connection.

It's not about how to stay or if you should, rather it's one woman's story of what it could look like if you choose to or want to or must, for now. It's about growing faith and knowing ourselves and what it really means to be well. I'm so glad Annie finally wrote her stories of what it means to be rooted in a rootless world. Lucky you that you get to read it now for the very first time.

—Emily P. Freeman, *New York Times* bestselling author of
*How to Walk into a Room: The Art of Knowing
When to Stay and When to Walk Away*

# A Note on Staying Put

I am someone who stays.

When I was eighteen, I had dreams of becoming a journalist and moving to New York. It was the era of the writerly romcom; you know the ones, where female protagonists have a story to tell, and the only place to tell it is from a bohemian New York apartment. Instead, I went to the smallest college you could possibly imagine, then planted my roots in a tiny town in the rural South, a speck on the map smaller than my hometown. I have not lived the adventurous life I envisioned for myself as a teenager; I have, against all odds and dreams to the contrary, chosen to stay, and in the staying, I believe there is a story to tell.

Of course, I didn't think there was. I have lived much of my life in the pages of books, and the novels I read are often set in big cities, in far-off places I visit on vacation before crashing back home where my front door sticks thanks to the oppressive humidity. I have read very few books about stayers; those stories don't have pulsating plotlines or climactic moments of courage. Those books are the quiet ones, your *Crossing to Safety*, your *Jayber Crow*. They are lauded for their quietness, but no critic says what we're really thinking, which is that these are the stories most familiar to our souls.

Most of us, as it turns out, stay. Among young adults, 80 percent live within one hundred miles of their hometown. Those bohemian apartments aren't affordable for most of us, so we stay: in our marriages, even when they're hard; in our jobs, even when we hope for more; in our towns, even when they're lonely; in our faith, even when we almost can't breathe from the pain of it.

We may even try our best to leave. I left my hometown for college, moving to a different state, expecting to become a different person. Most of my childhood friends, ironically, stayed put. I grew up in a college town, and to leave and attend a university elsewhere—particularly one so small and insignificant—was a mystery among my peers. I, on the other hand, had never even considered staying, and when I arrived at an unspectacular university on a strip of highway in Alabama, I wondered if I'd done the right thing after all.

For the entirety of my college career, I lived in the land of sweet tea and Alabama football, never quite understanding any of it, but assuming I might wind up staying forever. I'd fallen in love with a boy with a southern accent and roots so deep in the Alabama dirt I speculated I'd never be able to pull free, until law school and ambition and bills came calling, and we both wound up back in my hometown. I'd left, only to return—the worst outcome, a failure by the world's standards, perhaps, too, by mine.

Then, five years after living in cozy apartments nestled among oak trees, mere minutes from family and friends, my own adventure finally came calling. My husband and I had watched as our friends graduated from doctoral programs or with master's degrees, fleeing my transient hometown of Tallahassee, Florida, to begin new lives in Colorado and Kansas, Texas and Tennessee. We'd hosted goodbye parties and sent parting gifts, and now we hoped it was our turn. Our adventure, though, was just a short forty-five-minute trip up the highway, across the state line, into a tiny town in Georgia we'd visited only for date night.

Thomasville is a romantic town, if you visit on the right night. The sunsets are spectacular; pink and orange and purple streak across the sky behind water towers and church steeples. The brick roads are empty, and the streetlights blink lazily, and you think: *I could live here. I could call this quiet place under the stars home.*

So we did. We bought a bookstore and, subsequently, a life. We moved to a small town without an airport or an interstate, and on the right night, it's all still quite romantic.

Except, of course, when it's not.

Staying put requires a certain strength of imagination. You have to run outside to romanticize sunsets and smile at inconvenient but lengthy encounters in grocery stores. You have to count to ten and take deep breaths and list the reasons you've stayed: The affordability, the practicality, the legacy, the familiarity. The neighbor who knows your name, the coffee shop that knows your order. Staying isn't exactly as Wallace Stegner or Wendell Berry described it. It's more effort, more boredom, more be-content-with-your-contentedness than I really expected.

Staying means blooming where you're planted, a phrase I've always loved, but I admittedly loved it most when I thought I'd be planted in New York or Italy or the Cotswolds, or even a place like Savannah or Atlanta or Birmingham.

Instead, here I am. There you are.

My best friend moved away when I was twelve years old. She was our preacher's daughter, and we spent most of our Sunday afternoons together at someone's house before it was time to go back to church again on Sunday evening. I loved the freedom of those long and lazy afternoons, the spontaneity of wearing each other's clothes, roaming around outside, jumping in swimming pools, playing boarding school. (I suppose I have always had a wanderer's heart.)

I am not a dramatic person, but when I found out my friend was moving, I was devastated, tearful. I look back now and wonder if this was a moment when church became hard for me, if this memory looms larger than I want to give it credit for.

Nevertheless, we had one more Sunday afternoon together, and I have a distinct memory of standing atop her family's brick fireplace that Sunday, side by side and barefoot, performing Dolly Parton and Vince Gill's duet, "I Will Always Love You." A singer I am not, but I poured everything I had into that performance, always picking the lowest register so I had even the possibility of staying in tune. I wanted my friend to know how much I loved her. I wanted her to know I wouldn't forget her. I wanted her to stay, but if I couldn't make her stay, I wanted her to know *I would*. I'd remain faithful and loyal and true.

This is a book for the people who stayed, who sang their hearts out and threw goodbye parties and pretended to be happy when someone else announced their leaving. I've written stories for us, for the stayers, for the people who didn't fulfill their big-city dreams but whose lives have turned out bigger than they ever imagined. Stories for the in-betweeners, for those stuck in the muddy, messy middle, navigating relationships with people whom they no longer recognize, choosing to stay with them anyway. Stories for those of us whose faith is indelibly wrapped up in who we are and who we long to be, no matter how complicated or how isolated that faith leaves us feeling.

This isn't a tutorial on how to stay. It's not a guide to becoming friends with your neighbors or building relationships or living in a small town. Those books have already been written. Instead, this is a collection of stories about a life rooted in place, the blooming of possibility that can happen there, but also the hardship, the loneliness, the longing for more. I wanted stories that showed it all, because those are the stories so many of us are living. These stories are about bearing witness to the staying seasons and what we can learn when we choose or are forced to stay put.

PART I

# Staying Friends

*Everybody has a home team: It's the people you call when you get a flat tire or when something terrible happens. It's the people who, near or far, know everything that's wrong with you and love you anyways. These are the ones who tell you their secrets, who get themselves a glass of water without asking when they're at your house. These are the people who cry when you cry. These are your people, your middle-of-the-night, no-matter-what people.*

—Shauna Niequist, *Bread and Wine*

# CHAPTER I

# The Art of the Goodbye Party

One Christmas, Jordan gifted me a pineapple ornament to put on our tree. Pineapples, we'd learned during some museum tour or another, signified hospitality, and it was true: over the course of that year, we had hosted people in our home week after week, for book club meetings and small groups and dinner parties and Friendsgivings and craft nights and awards shows.

We were in our mid-twenties, and we were determined to have friends. We would not be like the millennials on the internet, pining for something they couldn't have, and I refused to have moved back home only to befriend the people I'd known in high school. I wanted the much-sought-after-but-ever-elusive adult friendship. I read a book called *MWF Seeking BFF*, and I said yes to random lunches with coworkers, and despite my profound introversion, over the years I found my people. My adult, grown-up people.

It's one of the things I'm proudest of my younger self for doing.

It would have been easy in those early years of marriage to focus solely on Jordan, on our relationship, on our marriage, but Jordan was finishing up law school. He was busy. His people were not my people. I'm glad I didn't get completely consumed by our marriage. We were so young, and I could have. Instead, I had to build relationships outside of my husband. I think it made our marriage healthier; I know it made my friendships more vibrant and lasting.

And then, the year after the pineapple, our friends, one by one, began to move. This, the literature had not prepared me for. The authors I read wrote about friendships spanning decades, neighborhood Halloween parties where the kids grew up on the same block, lifelong relationships built in those first years of marriage that continued to blossom ad infinitum. I thought we had more time. I thought we had an unspoken rule. Was no one reading the same books I was? We were in a book club together, for crying out loud! Didn't we all agree this life was the one we'd always wanted?

Tallahassee, it turns out, is a transient town. I didn't realize it because it's my hometown. I didn't move there for college; I was born there. My parents never left. I figured if I eventually made my way back—a decision I initially hated—I'd probably stay, too, especially if I built a community I loved. Many of my high school classmates were still around, so it was shocking to me when the women I'd befriended in adulthood slowly began to leave. Husbands got jobs elsewhere. Friends earned their doctorates.

I couldn't figure it out. Weren't the parties and the gatherings I'd hosted incentives to stay? Jobs were worth moving for, sure, but weren't friendships worth staying for? Friends are hard to find in adulthood; everybody says so. Once you've found your people, why would you leave them? I never presumed I'd be the person who threw goodbye parties and waved metaphorical handkerchiefs from the metaphorical shore. I presumed we'd all remain on shore together, or, maybe, if I was lucky, I'd be the one on the boat.

The year after the pineapple became the year of the goodbye party.

Each time our friends told us they'd be leaving, Jordan and I both kicked into gear. Rejoice with those who rejoice, even when it makes you want to vomit and punch a hole in the wall? Absolutely. We refused to wallow, pushed grief to a different compartment in our brains. We'd cry later. For now, we were thrilled! Happy for every friend making a new life decision, moving all over the country. One couple left for Texas. Then the next to Colorado, and the next to Jacksonville. Three "couple friends" in our twenties had felt like an embarrassment of riches. It was the stuff my grown-up dreams were made of! But when all three moved within a matter of months, I realized how few of us there actually had been.

My single friends left, too. Rachel, who, like me, had moved back home after college, left for Nashville. I was devastated. She was a remnant of the past, my best friend in my former life and also my current one. I didn't want her to go, but I didn't want her to stay, either. I wanted her to go find her next best, beautiful thing. I would never want to hold anyone I loved back. So she went, and I stayed.

When my friend Mandy graduated with her doctorate, she

announced she'd be moving to Chicago. We went out to dinner to celebrate, and I wondered if I'd ever see her again.

Then my brother moved.

Befriending my brother when I moved back to my hometown had been a bonus, a surprise. He was finishing up his degree at Florida State University (do you notice a pattern? Readers who live in college towns, beware), so when Jordan and I moved, he became a friend. He'd come over to our house for lunch or dinner or to watch *Arrested Development*. When I started to pursue my graduate degree, he'd drive me to the campus so I wouldn't have to find parking. I was living in a sitcom, and I took it for granted.

My mother is one of eight siblings, five of whom still live within a ten-mile radius from one another. I didn't necessarily expect myself or my brother to live in Tallahassee forever, but when we both found ourselves there in our twenties, I made assumptions. We'd have, I guessed, what my mother had always had: our future children would grow up down the street from their cousins. We'd have each other forever.

When he announced he was moving—again, to Nashville, what was going on up there?—I didn't understand. Him, too? I look back now and realize: Of course. We were all in our twenties. The homes we'd made were never supposed to be permanent.

Permanence is for your thirties, your forties. But I got married at twenty-two. Those books I was reading were written by authors in middle age (your Jen Hatmakers, your Shauna Niequists). All my life I had been a late bloomer, but I was ready to settle far earlier than my other friends were. I'd found Jordan, and then I'd built a community, and I figured: *This is it. This is all I needed.*

It didn't occur to me that for most of my adult friends, Tallahassee was only ever meant to be the starting point.

I celebrated each milestone and achievement because my friends were worthy of it. I threw one last Galentine's Day shindig—those were my favorite—and I look back on that night with tenderness, because I know I was sad. I'm sad writing about it. That year was hard, brutal.

Hard because goodbyes are hard, but also because people's life changes make you start to examine your own. If everyone around you were leaving, wouldn't that make you wonder why you were staying? When we talk about goodbyes, or milestones, or cross-country moves, we don't want to articulate the jealousies bubbling up inside us. I didn't want to admit it then and don't want to admit it now, but part of the reason I threw parties and went to dinners was to quiet the jealous voices in my head.

When Jordan graduated from law school, we both knew it was "my turn." I'd financially supported and held up our family during his law school years and put off my own graduate work. Once he graduated, I applied to grad schools: Alabama, Georgia, FSU, Georgetown (admittedly, a long shot). Jordan applied to judicial clerkships, too: DC. New York. Maybe we could live our big-city dreams after all.

But I didn't get accepted to Georgetown. Jordan didn't get the clerkships we'd dreamed were possible. I could choose among Alabama, Georgia, and Florida—the story, it turns out, of my life.

We chose to stay, mostly for our marriage. If I went to Alabama or Georgia, Jordan's job possibilities meant long commutes. We'd never see each other, so I attended grad school in Tallahassee for one semester before I realized it wasn't for me. I quit.

We'd had our chance to leave, and we hadn't taken it. And our options had never looked like the options of our friends. Tuscaloosa, Athens, Tallahassee. The South. Always the South. The rest of our friends were moving to metropolitan areas near major airports: a dream! Boulder. Chicago. Kansas City. Dallas. Nashville. Even Jacksonville all of a sudden sounded like an adventure.

It did not feel like an adventure to stay.

The goodbye parties, then, were an act of resistance against my own melancholia. At its best, jealousy can point us in the direction of our heart's longings. At its worst, it can fester, boil over, ruin relationships, lead to bitterness, defensiveness. *If this town is good enough for me, why isn't it good enough for you?*

If my early twenties taught me about friend-making, my late twenties taught me how to start over, how to wish people well, how to say goodbye. It's a lesson I'm grateful I learned relatively early, because, in life, people are always leaving. Have you noticed?

Perhaps it's my southern sensibility, but I'd long taken for granted a rootedness in people. I did not grow up moving; my parents' jobs were relatively stable, straightforward. We once moved to a new home with a larger yard five miles down the road, and I thought my life had ended. That's how rooted we were.

Now everyone moves, constantly. Moves to be closer to grandparents and the free childcare. Moves for a job. Moves into a bigger place. Moves for a fresh start, making me wonder if my life will be stale if I stay.

I am no longer in my twenties. I am rapidly approaching forty. I do not have children. We do not live in a neighborhood surrounded by lifelong friends and their little ones on Halloween night. There are no Fourth of July barbecues, and the Galentine's Day brunches are smaller than they used to be. It sometimes feels like I was sold a false bill of goods, promised something that doesn't actually exist outside of television or movies. Except, I think for some people, it does.

After our friends left, we moved, too, to a small town where families have lived for generations, where houses are known by the family name of whoever lived there last. ("Oh! You just bought the Smiths' house! Good for you!") I watch, and I see people who have exactly what I wanted in those early years, and my old jealousies percolate.

But then I think I am the perfect person to live here, to welcome my fellow from-aways and provide them a soft place to land. I know what it's like to move to a small town where you'll never quite fit, and I also know what it's like to live in your hometown. I know what it's like to want to find friends outside of your childhood experience. There are challenges to both leaving and staying, and I'd like to think I'm equipped to handle them all, capable of showing other people the way.

Because of all the goodbyes from that year, I now hold relationships with an open hand. It is easier, comes more naturally, to be happy when people leave. I have a lot of practice.

While I was writing this book, two of my closest friends announced they were moving. When they told me, I did not hesitate in my happiness for them. My twenties made that happiness possible. I was also deeply sad. I did not want to write a book about staying while watching more people leave. I do not want to be the last one standing, do not want to be in my forties still chasing the community I built for myself twenty years ago.

Life, though, isn't always like the books we read. It's messier. I can be happy for my friends while also feeling sorry for myself. I can wish them well on their next adventures while quietly pining for my own. I can do this, in part, because I've stayed close to my friends as they each started their new chapters, and did you know it rains in Boulder? There is traffic in Dallas, and bad days exist in Nashville and Greensboro the same as they do here.

I still experience whispers of jealousy at a friend's goodbye. But mostly I wish them well, and we stay in touch, because life is too short and my friendships are too good to let time zones get in the way. I talk to my long-distance friends just as much as—maybe more than—my local ones, and our connectedness keeps me grounded and rooted, just like I always wanted.

We do not live in the same neighborhood, but a sidewalk isn't the only thing that can connect you to your people. Having friends all over the country has loosened my grip, in all the best ways. I no longer exude proprietary force over my relationships. My friends live their adventures, and I live mine. Because it's all adventure, leaving and staying, and we'll all do a little bit of both over the courses of our lives. We'll get better at it with practice.

Now, every Christmas, Jordan and I hang the pineapple ornament on our tree with gratitude and fondness for the year we spent opening our home and celebrating our friends. There is a bittersweetness to it, but I wouldn't trade it. I'm glad to have a glittering, tangible reminder of what we had, what we've lost, and what we've fought to keep.

# CHAPTER 2

# Boot-Scootin' Boogie

I was in a stressful season. It was the fall of 2019, and changes to my work as an independent bookstore owner were on the horizon. (So was a pandemic, but I didn't know that then.) My mastermind group—a group of five women from various corners of the South, most of them, somewhat oddly, therapists—had just met for the first time in Birmingham, where we'd been discussing our careers and entrepreneurship. Most of us were, in some form or fashion, exhausted. The phrase we kept repeating aloud to ourselves was something to the effect of "But I'm also a person."

As in "I'm in charge of this business, but I'm also a person."

"I'm a boss, but I'm also a person."

"I feel like I keep making mistakes," to which the couch full of therapists would reply, "But you're just a person!"

As we reflected upon our collective and individual humanity and the ways in which it made an impact on our work, we talked a little about play. Did we do anything for fun? In starting or running our businesses, had we forgotten our personhood, the childhood versions of ourselves? What could we do as hobbies without turning them into side hustles?

It was a question that plagued me when I got home. Like many millennials, I'd turned my primary act of enjoyment (reading) into a career. I still loved to read—books have never lost their pleasure for me—but I also didn't consider curling up in a chair for hours on end particularly playful. I was worried I didn't know how to play anymore, so over the months I embarked on a one-woman mission to play.

When experts and journalists and academics write about the concept of play in adulthood, the importance of doing something for nothing, they frequently mention a common theme: do what you did when you were younger. "When you were a child, what were your favorite ways to play?" asked author and former schoolteacher Meredith Sinclair (*Well Played*) in a piece with the *New York Times* back in 2020. "And when was the last time you had these same types of feelings as an adult? What current activities bring you close to that same unabashed feeling you had as a youngster?"

I was a creative kid with an interest in—though not the body or athleticism for—sports, so in my year of play, I bought watercolors, kicked around a soccer ball, swam, served a volleyball to myself, learned Taylor Swift songs on the piano, swung in the swings in the park across from my house. I played, but it didn't feel playful. I wondered if it was because I was doing all these things alone.

No one bore witness to my playing, so it felt like it didn't count, like it wasn't real.

And then, about a year after that mastermind meeting, just as the weather started to turn, a friend from my book club invited me to her line dancing class at the YMCA.

I don't know why I said yes to Julie Anna's invitation. It's not at all the kind of thing I would typically say yes to. I am a person who knows herself intimately. I know what I am capable of and what I am not, and I am not capable of rhythm. And it's fine! You can go through life, and rhythm might never come up. You'll look a little silly dancing at weddings, but who doesn't? I wonder, though, if my months of attempted play had, perhaps, prepared me for a yes, primed me for a little bit of silliness.

At the time, Julie Anna and I had interacted almost exclusively through our book club. We'd gone on a couple of lunches together, but we weren't Anne-and-Diana, bosom friends. I am a goofy person, but only the people I love and trust the very most get to see the goofiest parts of me. Line dancing without rhythm would require a level of goof Julie Anna had not yet seen, but for whatever reason—I suppose because of the months of attempted play that preceded it—I said I'd go. To a class at the Y. Sometimes I can still surprise myself.

So one October evening, I left the comfort of my cozy home and ventured to the Y, where I placed myself behind Julie Anna and beside Courtney, another book club friend and recent line dancing convert. I was nervous when I walked in, but a glance around the room showed me we were the youngest attendees by at least two decades, maybe three. I am at my most comfortable around the elderly, so I immediately felt at ease.

I stumbled all over myself in that first class—several fellow students seemed deeply concerned for my welfare—but I had an absolute blast. I loved being bad at something but trying anyway. I loved no expectations and no judgments and no one really paying me any mind. I loved laughing with my friends and jumping with excitement when I finally got a move right.

There's an early episode of *Friends* where Monica, Phoebe, and Rachel find themselves in a tap class. Rachel takes to it, of course, like a fish to water, nailing every move with almost no effort. Monica tries hard but cannot seem to grasp it: "I'm not getting this!" she yells to her friends. Phoebe moves to her own beat, waving her hands in the air with complete disregard. "I'm *totally* getting it!" she yells back.

I am Monica, but buried right under the surface is Phoebe. Learning to play—kicking around that soccer ball, swimming in my pool, painting outside the lines—brought her out of me, and by the time I got to line dancing class, I *almost* didn't care that I was bad. I didn't find it mattered. Playing was silencing the perfectionist inside me, and I was hooked.

At least once a week, I'd join my friends for class. Julie Anna, a former swing dancer, had rhythm I hadn't known she possessed. She'd stand in front of me each class and inconspicuously point so I'd know which direction to go and when. (I say I have no rhythm, but truthfully it might be coordination that's actually the problem. At weddings, when it's time for the electric slide, nine times out of ten I'm sliding the wrong way.) Julie Anna was my saving grace, and Courtney was, too. Sometimes other friends from book club would join us as we boot-scooted our way across the shiny floor, and week after week, our friendship became more and more solid-ified, intimate.

My years in Thomasville had been hard, friendship-wise. I'd done such a good job of building friendships in Tallahassee. I'd graduated from college, moved back home, and made it my mis-sion to find "grown-up" friends. Thanks to work and book club and church, I did. The women I met in those Tallahassee years are still some of my best friends. We're spread all over the country, but we text and voice message and plan trips together. They are my lifeline.

Perhaps because I'd done such a good job of maintaining my older friendships, I struggled in Thomasville to make new ones. I couldn't figure out how to meet people outside of the bookstore I'd purchased; I was there all the time. I started a book club, but it took a couple of years before it became solid. Members came and went, and I wasn't the most reliable version of myself. I'd always prided myself on my loyalty, my steadfastness, my ability to show up for my friends, but one morning, a new acquaintance texted "Where are you?" and I realized I'd forgotten our breakfast. I'd never written it down anywhere, and I'd unintentionally stood her up. I'd done damage that wasn't reparable so early in a relationship, and I hated it.

I threw myself into the bookstore; I felt like I had to in order to make it work. Friendship could no longer be a top priority. I didn't have the capacity for it. So in those early years of my Bookshelf tenure, I found myself befriending fellow staffers. I was twenty-seven. I didn't know where else to turn. I spent most of my time with the people on staff, and at previous jobs, I'd befriended my fellow employees. The difference, of course, was now I was the boss, their boss, so close friendship wasn't really appropriate. It was always going to backfire.

Julie Anna's invitation felt like a lifeline, a chance to build friendships beyond monthly book club meetings and away from staffers trying to do their jobs. My favorite friendships have always been the close-knit ones, the intimate ones, but those require time, and in adulthood, time is our most finite resource; it's the one thing we feel like we don't have. Monthly meetings weren't resulting in the close-knit relationships I craved, but daily work was, and it was complicating my own work as an employer and business owner. My friendship scales were off-balance. Long-distance friendships are lovely and life-giving, but proximity matters. I needed friends who were actually here, in body as well as in spirit.

Those weekly classes where we sweat to Meghan Trainor and "Wagon Wheel" began to tip the scales back in my favor. Dancing made me a better boss, a better version of myself, a better in-person friend. A weekly commitment of my time meant I was more open to saying yes to movie nights, to dinners out. I didn't know what I was missing until I had it again, and all it took was one invitation, and one yes.

In the early months of 2020, before Covid became a real threat, Julie Anna confessed she'd never seen the classic American film

*Clueless,* so our friend group immediately scheduled a movie night to rectify the error. But a couple of days before our *Clueless* watch party, Julie Anna and Courtney saw a flier at the YMCA.

### LINE DANCERS!
### JAMBOREE DANCE AT SEAPLANE OPRY HOUSE
### SOUTH OF MOULTRIE

Somehow then, when Friday night rolled around, instead of relaxing on one of our couches to watch Paul Rudd become Paul Rudd, the three of us wound up in Courtney's 2012 Jetta and headed to meet the rest of our line dancing classmates at the Seaplane Opry House.

We drove along the pitch-black backroads of South Georgia, my nausea growing with every turn. I was brave and playful enough to enjoy line dancing in front of the mirrored walls of a gym classroom, but the real-life dancing scenario we were about to encounter had me on edge. *Maybe we won't find it,* I thought, fondly remembering Alicia Silverstone and Julie Anna's big, comfy couch. But then, in the distance, we spotted colorful Christmas lights and a slew of cars. My calm gummies kicked in, and we laughed and giggled nervously as we approached the door, my friends in their cowboy boots and me in my Keds. I'd never even been to a club.

As we entered, to the left of the door were church tables all lined with chairs facing one direction. Paper plates were filled with fried chicken and pimento cheese, and the average age of the people seated had to be sixty-five. It felt a little like a church fellowship hall, except under red twinkle lights and a giant disco ball was a dance floor, and up on a stage was a live band called the Southern Comforts.

I felt like we'd opened the wardrobe door into Narnia.

Outside, it was cold and dark and January. The world was burning, literally and figuratively.

But inside, it was warm, and there was dancing, and no one cared who we were or why we were there or what was happening in the rest of the world.

Inside, George Strait and Hank Williams still reigned supreme. Couples who looked like they'd been there since the '70s dotted the dance floor, and there, in the very front, were our YMCA classmates.

For nearly three hours, we watched and danced and laughed and marveled. We joked about the sacredness of the space, only it wasn't funny, not really. I finally understood Pam Beesly's infamous "I feel God in this Chili's tonight" because God really *is* at Chili's, and on dance floors, and in honky-tonks.

We walked into that room, and everyone was exactly who they were, no pretenses, no airs, no judgments. I didn't need to worry about my Keds, or my wool sweater, or not fitting in, or messing up steps, because no one was paying attention. They were too busy having fun.

There was freedom under that disco ball, I swear.

Somewhat surprisingly, all the moves I'd been learning in class translated to the actual dance floor. Sure, there was the occasional misstep, a hip bump or shoulder touch with a stranger, but again: no one cared, including me. I was Phoebe.

As the dance floor began to clear, we headed to the car, breathless with joy. I felt outside of my body while also being completely aware of it. We found a '90s country playlist on Spotify, and all the way back to Thomasville, we blared John Michael Montgomery and Reba, singing at the top of our lungs. I felt sixteen again, but with none of the angst and a little more wisdom.

We repeatedly tried to replicate the magic of that Friday night in January, and for a while, it worked. We went to a high school gymnasium in a small North Florida town, where we danced and I won a Ziploc bag of kumquats during the nightly raffle. (A sentence I never thought I'd type.) We found ourselves in the oddest places, line dancing with our older friends from class, and shoring up our own friendship for the years to come.

I don't know what would have happened if the pandemic hadn't happened. Would we have line danced forever? Would I still be doing the Cleveland Shuffle on Monday nights, sweating and laughing, high on endorphins and Brad Paisley's "Toothbrush"?

I doubt it. Life happens, and in this case, Covid happened. Our line dancing classes came to an end, and although we discovered the weekend dances at various opry houses continued, we didn't attend. We worried about our older friends. We didn't want to get anyone sick. Some of our political and cultural differences with those in our class became more evident, and those fissures felt bigger than they once did.

But my friendship with Julie Anna and Courtney continued.

Line dancing had cemented it. During the pandemic, we had outdoor picnics. We celebrated birthdays with presents dropped off on stoops. We hosted Zoom book clubs and Netflix watch parties. We took long, looping walks. I no longer relied upon the bookstore staff to give me the relationships I needed. I kept in touch with my long-distance friends, but now I had in-town friends, too. I discovered how crucial to my existence it was to have people in my literal corner. The internet has introduced me to some truly lovely souls over the years. I am loyal to the people I have known forever, and I cling to my faraway friends. But I am so grateful for friends I can see and touch and hug, who I sit next to in the movie theater, who I karaoke in cars with, who I dig toes into the sand with. Geography matters.

In-person friends bear witness to the more mundane ins and outs of our lives. We need them. I need them. The pandemic taught me that. Sleazy sliding (an actual line dancing move and now the official name of our group chat) taught me that.

Thanks be to God. And Brooks & Dunn.

# CHAPTER 3

# Nothing like Old Friends

Every few months, on a Monday night, I drive the tree-lined highway between Thomasville and Tallahassee, back toward my hometown. I'm not running my "big-city" errands to Trader Joe's and Target; no, that task is reserved for a quiet morning or afternoon. Instead, I'm doing what most millennial women do for fun on a weeknight: I'm meeting a friend for dinner.

These occasional dinners are different from the ones I attend in Thomasville. In Thomasville, I'm having dinner with women I've known for a few years, with girls from my book club and the women in my YMCA class. We're talking about our marriages, our breakups, the funny things their children say on the way to school. We split appetizers and talk about our workdays and what we hope might come next. We share television show recommendations and add songs to our Spotify playlists and books to the TBR lists we keep in our Notes apps. We laugh, and we listen, and we make plans for next time. In between, we'll inevitably run into one another at church or in the bookstore or at the grocery store. We are neighbors, committed and cemented in this small-town existence together. These are the women who know the present-day version of me, and I am glad for them. I fought for them.

My dinners in Tallahassee, though, are not fueled by my present tastes or my daily routines so much as they are fueled by nostalgia. There is little talk of my life as a bookstore owner; there is little discussion of work or livelihood at all. Instead, I sit down with Morgan, whom I've known since I was eight, and we talk about who we used to be.

Years ago, back when I filled my lengthy office days with reading strangers' journal entries on the internet, I came across a blogger who continually referred to her best friend as "best-friend-Jenny-since-I-was-six." It was occasionally obnoxious, but in an adorable way, and before I got too jealous at such a feat of friendship, I realized I, too, had a best friend I'd known for that long.

Morgan and I met when we were in the second grade; we became the kind of friends who are a little bit inseparable, the kind of friends who have plans scheduled for every weekend, plans that probably involve a slumber party. We played in a Saturday-morning basketball league on a team coached by my dad, and I'd go over to her house, and she'd come over to mine. We'd play with our dolls, pretend to be away at boarding school, shoot hoops on the goal in my driveway. She had a glamorous older sister; I had a pesky but funny younger brother. Together, we had the best of both worlds.

The first and only time I ever used a Ouija board, I was with Morgan. I, in turn, introduced her to *Jaws*, insisting we fast-forward and rewind *to*, not *through*, all the bloody parts. I know she has a long white scar on her right thigh from the time she fell on a rusty nail while we were babysitting some neighbor's kids. She tearfully went to urgent care, and I got stuck babysitting a bunch of rambunctious toddlers. My most distinct childhood memories are wrapped up in Morgan.

On the cusp of our teenage years, we grew apart. Nothing dramatic happened; there was no blowup, no fight, no disagreement I can recall. Her parents were getting divorced, and twenty-five years later, I wonder if that caused the distance between us. But I was thirteen, so I didn't psychoanalyze or perform a relationship autopsy. I only felt a little dejected, a little lonely. Morgan had found other friends, so I did, too. That's what you do when you're thirteen.

Then, two years later, in the middle of high school, Morgan came calling. My mother still brings it up nearly every time I'm home, says it's one of the most courageous things she's ever witnessed. My friend came back, said she missed me, said she wanted us to be friends again. Even at fifteen, Morgan was so clear and honest about her desires, vulnerable before Brené Brown taught us what vulnerability is. My mother is, of course, right. It was an adult act of bravery before we were even remotely adult.

We renewed our friendship. We giggled and laughed and made up. We'd go to her house for off-campus lunch, trade inside jokes during yearbook class. We bought fake glasses so we could look more like the serious writers and journalists we wanted to be, then got headaches wearing them to the movie theater. We went to our school's senior banquet together; when another friend kicked me out of my hotel room during our class senior trip, Morgan let me sleep on her couch. I helped her move into her first apartment.

Morgan stayed in Tallahassee for college, and whenever I came back home, we'd try to grab coffee or lunch, whatever it took to keep our friendship intact. It's like we'd learned from our preteen selves and didn't want any past mistakes to repeat themselves. She met Jordan on one of those visits home and proclaimed he looked just like Matthew McConaughey, back when Matthew McConaughey was at his most handsome. Like me, Morgan was raised on the romantic comedies of the 1990s and 2000s; this was the highest praise she could offer, and I knew it. Years later, she stood beside me on my wedding day. Young and broke and moving into our first place, Jordan and I inherited her hand-me-down TV and a dresser set she'd bought from Goodwill. I still have the mirror from that set in our bedroom today. I can't bear to part with it, this physical reminder of a friend I've known all my life, a friend who'd look at my youth, my inexperience, and say, "Here. Have my dresser."

For a while, Morgan and I were like ships passing in the night. I lived in Tallahassee during my initial years of marriage, but Morgan didn't. She'd moved away right when I moved back. It was sad at first, to live in my hometown without my hometown best friend. But I made other friends. She did, too. We talked on the phone some; I helped plan her sister's wedding, tried, briefly, to set her up with a guy I thought she might like. We weren't necessarily best friends anymore, by the traditional, elementary school definitions, but we also never lost touch. When she moved back to Tallahassee with her husband, I was living in Thomasville, so we started going to dinner, and when we sit across from each other, no matter how long it's been, it feels like no time has passed at all.

I love that we know each other's family members only by their respective honorifics: "How's Aunt Dottie?" "Tell Uncle Ray I said hello." I love that we know each other's past selves better than our present ones, that that knowledge somehow is the glue holding our friendship together, making our relationship work. I tell Morgan about my present life, sure, but I don't need her to know the ins and outs of my days. She knows me—the past me, the younger me—and it turns out, that's enough. That understanding gives her insight into my present way of being.

My text thread with Morgan isn't filled with book recommendations or inside jokes. It's startlingly sparse. There's the occasional reminder about dinner, well-wishes for a birthday, and then, suddenly, an announcement about someone we mutually love who has died. Her granddad, my uncle. It's friendship at its most stripped down and bare.

The friends I've made in adulthood are blessings, but they are work: texts and DMs and the aforementioned dinners. I have failed at many of them, dropped balls, skipped lunches, missed birthdays. New friends become gracious with time—I've experienced this to be true—but they don't start that way. We're all trying to figure out who each other is, where we came from, what makes us tick. Old friends already know these things, so the expectations are different, lighter. There's a mutual understanding and grace.

Childhood friends don't necessarily know you best. I know this. But they do know a version of you best, and that can be such a relief in the harsh reality of adult life; sometimes we need someone who we don't need to explain ourselves to.

In my thirties, I've watched my friend become a wife, a mother, a caregiver to her aging father, a grieving daughter after his death. She's modeled for me things I haven't done yet myself, and when the time comes, I know I'll go to Morgan to remind me of what I have to do.

Living near your hometown comes with a fairly continuous series of existential crises; around every corner is the ghost of my former self, and I'm not always in the mood to greet her. A relationship with my childhood best friend is what makes those existential crises worth it.

My husband, who lives five hours from his hometown, doesn't keep in touch with his childhood best friends. At best, they are memories, faces on a screen, Facebook statuses, and Christmas card updates.

There are perils to living near your hometown, yes, but the perk is a childhood friend you watch become a grown-up. It's a lifetime of friendship and understanding sitting across from you at dinner. It's her running into your father at the drugstore and calling him "Dad."

I may not always live in Thomasville. Morgan may not always live in Tallahassee. For now, though, we are geographically inter-twined, and I'll gladly brave the ghosts of my former self to have Monday-night dinner with an old friend.

CHAPTER 4

# Book Club

Before there were midweek dinners out or weekend excursions to small-town honky-tonks, there was book club.

My first book club was a New Year's resolution I made when I was twenty-three, a resolution for years I bragged I'd actually seen to fruition. I didn't know how to meet people or make friends after college graduation, but I knew with Jordan in law school, I'd need company. I had made one friend through work—that's all it takes, just one—so when I set the goal in January to launch a book club, I asked her to join me. We tasked ourselves with inviting a handful of acquaintances from our respective churches and workplaces and neighborhoods, and it was like that baseball movie men love so much; we built it, and people came.

I can't remember the first book we read (just kidding; I looked it up, and it was, I am sorry to say, *The Shack*), but I know that first group we brought together never again had the same configuration. Women came and went all the time; I can't recall some of their names, cannot begin to picture all of their faces. Over our years of meeting, a core group of women eventually emerged, and a few of those became what I'd consider lifelong friends. We've stayed in touch across various moves and time zones, and although we still share book recommendations back and forth, our friendships have evolved into so much more. For so long, I thought *that* was the lasting legacy of my Tallahassee book club: I really did meet and make some of my very best friends through our monthly conversations.

But the older I get and the further removed I am from that original book club, the more I wonder if its primary long-term impact was actually a life lesson about hospitality and lowering expectations, the life-altering realization that surface relationships—relationships I once deemed shallow or unimportant—are the stuff of life. Settling for seemingly shallow relationships might be what saves us.

In other words, what if we just let book club be book club?

Even if you're the academic sort, book clubs should be a relatively low-stakes enterprise. Part of the reason women felt comfortable swimming in and out of the waters of our book club meetings was because as long as you'd read the book—or part of it, or a synopsis online—you could contribute to the conversation. Book clubs provide a low point of entry. You don't need to be an expert or an extrovert, the most well-spoken or the most intellectual. You can just sit and eat the snacks if you want. (Book clubs should always have snacks.) There's a point of commonality, and it has nothing to do with where you're from or what your degree is in or where you went to school or whether you're married or have children. It's just: Did you read the book? Why or why not? Did you like the book? Why or why not?

It's so easy to overcomplicate relationships and the effort they require. Book club simplifies all of it. When I moved to Thomasville, it took me months to let go of my old book group. I loved those women, even as the group had morphed and changed into something new and different. When there were more unfamiliar faces in the room than familiar, I knew it was time to plant my roots in my new community, and after living in Thomasville for about a year, I started a new book club in my new town. I'm not sure if any of the women who were at that first meeting are in the group today; that's how much a group can shift and change over the years.

I remember, though, that after months of trying to prove myself in this new place, I was relieved to just sit and talk about a common text; I didn't have to share about where I'd come from or who I'd been. I didn't really have to talk about The Bookshelf or why we'd moved. I just had to talk about ideas, characters, plotlines. That, I thought, I could do. No vulnerability hangover required.

It's true: I've met my best friends through book club. I think it's partly just the regularity of it; after meeting month after month for years, it's possible to eventually form bonds beyond the literary. In Tallahassee, those women came together for baby and bridal showers, goodbye dinners and support groups. Book club, I once told Jordan, felt like what I imagined church could be, a group of very different people from very different backgrounds and with very different interests and worldviews gathering in people's homes, swapping silly stories, and sharing in engagements and broken dates and favorite movies and promotions and pets.

But it's also just way lower stakes than that. Again, there were women in my book club whose names I can't remember. I couldn't name for you without looking at a spreadsheet (naturally, there is a spreadsheet) all the books we read.

Some months in book club, yes, we learn about a friend's breakup or we rejoice in the news of a new baby or a new marriage or a new job, but most of the time it's sitting and talking about a book, and that's it. I leave, and I don't feel deep or sentimental about it. It's just something I do, and that's the point.

I am, perhaps you've noticed, a "best friend" kind of girl. I love staying and nestling deep into relationships, long-term. I have always felt most made for in-depth, years-long friendship; I mate for life, and I pride myself on it.

But monthly book club meetings have made me a better acquaintance. I'm better at small talk now, and even though I still get very sweaty at cocktail parties, if I'm seated next to you at some random dinner function or another, I'm probably better company than most. I didn't used to be. I really think book club taught me how.

Life isn't always decades-long friendships or midnight heart-to-hearts. A lot of life is just showing up, offering a smile or a quick wave, maybe just checking in for a minute or two. A lot of life is shallow.

I once found myself in conversation—at book club, I think—with a woman I barely knew. I had just moved to Thomasville and was asking how she suggested meeting people. "I do weekly Bunco games in my neighborhood," she told me. "It's not like those women are necessarily going to become my best friends. But now I can wave and ask about their kids. It's nice."

This is where I've always struggled. Maybe it's my personality or my calendar or how I set boundaries or what I'm willing to do with my time. But this aspect of friendship and community is where I have always had the most difficulty. I am not good with surface-level relationships.

In *Better Than Before*, author and podcaster Gretchen Rubin asks if we're openers or finishers; are we better at starting new things or wrapping things up? Jordan immediately identified me as a finisher, and it's true. I am great at finishing things. I meet deadlines; I conquer my goals. Give me a task, and I will see it through. I am a finisher.

But life requires a lot of opening. And I am not so good with the opening, the starting of something new.

Rubin may not have meant for her questions to apply to relationships, but I think the principle of opening versus closing is apt when we're talking about friendships in adulthood.

I have several friends who are great at meeting new people. They are comfortable inviting strangers into their homes; they are confident in conversation and adept at networking and small talk. They set people at ease and know how to be hospitable in their hearts and in their homes.

Those are things I become excellent at, with time. I have the potential to be a great friend. But I am not always a good acquaintance.

When I started my Thomasville book club, I told myself I wouldn't have high expectations, but I secretly hoped I'd meet a couple of kindred spirits, bosom friends, lifelong companions. The community I'd dreamed of would start building itself.

That is a lot of pressure to put on any one person or group, and I think my early years in Thomasville suffered from that pressure. I kept expecting my book club and some random women's group I'd joined to leave me with my new ride-or-dies, and I was constantly disappointed. It was so much more enjoyable to finally allow book club to be what it actually is: a fun monthly gathering of a group of people who talk about books. Period.

The woman who plays Bunco? She told me she had difficulty forming close friendships, but unlike me, she never seemed to mind. She's got Bunco. Book club. Maybe a small group through her church. Those relationships tend to be surface level by her admission, but they have the potential to grow into something more. And if they don't? They still count. She knows their names, their stories, can wave and visit and interact comfortably.

Surface, I have learned, might be okay. It might even be enough. It might be all there is.

I am not the perfect acquaintance, but book club has made me a better one. I am better at welcoming the stranger, waving at a random person I slightly recognize in the grocery store, smiling and chatting without going too deep, too fast. I have learned that although I adore my close-knit, lifelong friendships, I equally enjoy the dozens of neighbors and acquaintances I've met. What a revelation, to realize that while the world is telling us how important it is to have deep friends we can cherish for decades, it's sometimes okay to just sit with a bowl of Cheez-Its or Peanut M&M'S and talk about a book.

This is also more doable, more conducive to the lives we already have.

We might not have time to dig deep with an hours-long confessional, but I imagine we have one hour in the middle of our months to meet with a group of random people from our work, church, or neighborhood. It takes the pressure off, to realize not every person you meet is a potential best friend. They might be someone you forget in a decade's time. That doesn't make them unimportant. It makes them human, and you one, too.

I am an advocate for book clubs. I own a bookstore, so I have a vested interest in the matter. But I believe in book clubs not simply because book clubs sell books. I believe book clubs change minds; help us hold better, more earnest conversations; bring us closer to our neighbors and friends. But I also think they're just good icebreakers, offering a low-stakes starting point for relationships. Joining a book club could be, for us, what our grandmothers and mothers experienced when they joined the garden club or played bridge. (Most of the women I know who are in a garden club don't even garden, and I doubt they're very concerned with finding their next BFF.)

Let's take the pressure off ourselves and the people we meet. Let's allow surface to be enough. Let's play Bunco and read books and wave to one another across the grocery store and think: *This is all I ever wanted.*

PART II

# Staying Put

*A place belongs forever to whoever claims it hardest, remembers it most obsessively, wrenches it from itself, shapes it, renders it, loves it so radically that he remakes it in his own image.*

—Joan Didion, *The White Album*

CHAPTER 5

# Sweat Equity

When I was twenty-six years old, I had a quarter-life crisis. Jordan had just gotten back from an international trip, and I'd been left at home to stew in my thoughts. I was terrified thirty was on the horizon, and I felt like I hadn't done anything.

Adulthood can be a slap in the face to a formerly overachieving child. Whoops! Turns out I'm *not* good at everything I try, and in fact, most adults just sit at desks. They work. They parent. They love. The end.

Most of us are excruciatingly ordinary.

I see beauty in it now, but for years, I had chafed against this reality, quoting Timothy Keller's *Every Good Endeavor* to myself while also scrolling job postings in case something more exciting came along. I was employed at a legal association as a writer and editor, doing exactly what everyone said I'd never get to do when

I graduated with my journalism degree from a tiny Christian college. I was, actually, living the dream, just not the dream I'd always pictured. I got to take trips up the road to the state capitol, attend legal hearings that opened my eyes to injustice, interview lawmakers and state supreme court justices. It wasn't nothing. In fact, it was pretty great. But many days, I was bored.

When an indie bookstore announced its opening down the street from our rental home, I was thrilled. I loved bookstores, and this one had its flagship location in a tiny town just across the Florida-Georgia line. Jordan and I frequented there on date nights; I'd been to one of their store events for my birthday. Their location in Tallahassee would be smaller, situated inside a local cupcakery, and I couldn't believe my fortune. In Tallahassee, few neighborhoods are walkable to restaurants and shops, but this store would be within walking distance of our home, and visions of Nora Ephron's Kathleen Kelly began to float in my head.

I was thirteen when I saw Tom Hanks and Meg Ryan on the big screen, and although their love story has come under scrutiny in the modern era—a critique I personally do not share—everyone knows *You've Got Mail* is really about the bookstore.

The Shop Around the Corner dominated my imagination, and when Meg Ryan donned a princess hat and began reading to a group of enraptured children, I felt like one of them. *I could do that*, I thought, in awe of a possibility I'd never before considered.

So when I saw the bookstore I loved was opening a small outpost near me, I emailed the proprietor. I'd found her bio on their store website, and we had similar tastes in books, so I offered my

volunteer services: I'd host story time, come stock the shelves—
anything just to be inside a bookstore for an hour or two every
week.

The owner emailed me back, appreciative and thoughtful. She
wasn't hiring, but she was grateful for my support. A couple of
months later, I hosted my book club at the shop. I bought a copy
of *Gone Girl*.

I still have it, a first-edition hardback, and tucked inside,
there's a tiny business card from The Bookshelf's then owner.
The store's manager had recently resigned, and the owner now
wanted to interview me for the position. I was ecstatic, surprised.
Jordan and I were moving into a new home, and my mom recalls
me jumping up and down on my bed. Maybe I'd be somebody
before I turned thirty, after all. Maybe a bookstore would bring
meaning into my life.

In August 2012, I quit my secure journalism job (who knew
there was such a thing?) and began my work as a manager of the
little bookstore down the road from my house. It was as wonderful as I'd dreamed. I'd unlock the doors on a Tuesday morning and smell sugar in the air, see my co-workers icing cupcakes
while Brandi Carlile played on the speakers. At the time, we
mostly stocked children's books, so my mom and I began hosting midweek story times, and we'd read to little ones while their
own young moms took a breather. It was good, hard work, im-
bued with as much meaning as I'd predicted. I was no longer a
woman in crisis; I was a woman living out her purpose, finally.
Little in life is exactly what we hope it will be. I have no doubt

that season of my life held its challenges: our church experience was in upheaval, and I was working retail for the very first time, dealing with rude and irate customers and adjusting to a new work rhythm. But oh, how I loved it! I loved walking to work, loved the women who ran the cupcake shop, loved talking about books all day, loved setting up displays, loved incorporating my family into my work. It was just what I'd wanted, just the life I'd pictured, only in a different city from what I'd once imagined. I couldn't believe my good fortune.

As quickly as the dream began, it came crashing to an end. Nine months into my tenure as shop manager, the bookstore's owner informed me they'd be closing the store in Tallahassee and selling the store up the road in Thomasville. We engaged in countless entrepreneurial conversations and meetings; the dream became increasingly stressful as Jordan and I weighed our options and considered my passions. I loved my work, and one way to continue would be to buy the bookstore in Thomasville, an option the bookstore owner had suggested and encouraged. It felt ridiculous. I'd thought one day, maybe in retirement, I could *work* at a bookstore. I didn't think I'd be twenty-seven, didn't think the store would be in a small southern town, didn't think ownership was a possibility to consider. None of it made any practical or logical sense. I do not have entrepreneurship in my blood. This wasn't as easy a decision as managing the store had been. This decision would require a move, financial resources we didn't have, risk.

And then, a proposal. The owners of the bookstore, knowing

how reluctant Jordan and I were to take out loans, offered us the chance to buy the store through sweat equity, earning the store through my work.

All these years later, I'm still not exactly sure why they gave us this option. They'd had trouble selling the store; they were growing their family, and their entrepreneurial spirits seemed to be calling them on to their next project. But it was still a leap, risky for them, I know. It was risky for us, too, but I'm sure from an outsider's perspective their risk was greater. I wonder if they saw in us what might come next, if they had any inkling how seriously I'd take running their store, their town's store. I wonder if they somehow knew we were the right ones, so they offered me the same sort of deal Laban presented to Jacob in the Old Testament, The Bookshelf serving as my unwitting Rachel.

We signed on the dotted line. The contract wasn't perfect, and there were plenty of growing pains over the next few years. It is a struggle to own something only partially, to inherit something from someone who is more loved and more recognizable than you are. Small-business ownership is nothing I'd ever really recommend, and yet, we did it. Then, after five years of beginning to earn The Bookshelf (and, quite frankly, Thomasville's love), our contract was up. We could cut and run, our earnings turned into metaphorical dust. Or we could keep going. We could take out a small loan on the store's remaining purchase price, buy out the previous owners. The store could officially and financially be ours (and the bank's).

Another agonizing decision. The road to owning the store,

I now see, was full of them. I think everyone we loved figured we'd easily complete the buyout, but we were hesitant. Business contracts aren't sacrament, but I rarely go into anything lightly. Earning the store through sweat equity was a serious endeavor to me, buying it outright even more so. It felt permanent in a way I wasn't sure I was ready for; I still didn't even know if we liked Thomasville, or if it liked us. I loved the work, but we'd also made sacrifices. We didn't have children. We didn't make a lot of money. We didn't fit, really anywhere, though that probably wasn't The Bookshelf's fault.

But in June 2018, after watching Matt Damon buy a zoo, we bought a bookstore. (I am deeply concerned that my major life decisions are wrapped up in the pop culture I love.) Against all better judgment, we took out a business loan. The Bookshelf was ours. It was real now. It had always been real, to me. But now it was official to the world.

I recently found that first email I sent to the bookstore's owner, back when I was twenty-six. I cried reading it. My words were so sincere, so plain and earnest. I loved books, and I thought working in a bookstore would be a dream come true. That version of me never could have predicted the sleepless nights, the near-panic attacks, the human resources nightmares, the mean customers, the constant drowning in my own inadequacies. She was so blissfully unaware, and I am glad. Had she known any of it, she might have never sent the email at all.

She also never could have predicted the joys, the sense of

purpose and place, the kindness of customers, the treasured friendships, the utter happiness of unboxing new books and putting them on shelves. So much of bookstore ownership is nothing like the picture Nora Ephron painted for me. I do not wear a princess hat for story time, and I cry more than I ever did in the life I lived before.

This job has ripped me open; I'm not sure any other work I could have done would have done the same. I do not think I ever could have taken legal reporting nearly this personally.

Because, that's the truth of it. The work of The Bookshelf is so very personal, so wrapped up in who I am, in why I chose Thomasville, in why we continue to stay.

The bookstore is a dream come true. My friends know this, my family, Jordan. There are also days it is the stuff of nightmares, and I long to be bored behind a desk, just another cog in a bureaucratic machine. I long for the buck not to stop with me.

Business contracts are not sacrament, but my commitment to The Bookshelf does feel holy. The mission and meaning I searched for in the latter years of my twenties, I found. With it, there has come grief and stress and exhaustion. But I know I am lucky. I get to do, every day, what other folks only dream of doing. The magic of it—because there is a magic to it—is never lost on me.

Those early months of bookstore management in Tallahassee are still my favorite. It felt simpler, then. I sometimes wish I'd had longer in that season, wish I'd gotten to enjoy it a bit more before the added burden of shop ownership and the occasional cynicism that comes with it.

But I'm also exceedingly glad I said yes, took the risk, and made the leap. When Jordan and I were considering all of it, I went out to breakfast with my dad; I wanted to know what he thought. "You're too young to make a mistake," he told me. He gave me permission to try, and that is all I am doing, even still, all these years later. Trying. Failing. Succeeding. All the above.

# CHAPTER 6

# Stars Hollow & Sunsets

For a while, in the middle of our "Do we buy this bookstore?" decision-making process, I commuted between Tallahassee and Thomasville. We were still renting our home in Tallahassee, down the street from the now-closed bookstore where I thought I'd work forever—or at least longer than a year. That season of life had been happy but brief, and now Jordan and I both felt a little stuck. I was working in Thomasville, earning the flagship bookstore through sweat equity, but it was becoming more and more apparent how necessary it might be to live there, too. The commute wasn't bad, and Jordan still had his job in the downtown of the capital city, but I realized earning a small-town community's trust might mean uprooting our lives even further.

Jordan and I were both working late at the store together one Sunday night when we stepped outside to lock up. As I was bolting the door, Jordan glanced up and down the empty brick street, then looked at the sky. "It's so quiet here," he said. "You can see all the stars!"

And you could. I looked up and saw the glow of tiny sparkling stars against the backdrop of a deep black sky. The historic WPAX radio tower, with its blinking red letters. The streetlights glowing, not a car on the street but ours. We looked at each other, and we knew: this could be home.

Nothing else had convinced us. No dinner with friends, no well-intentioned bookstore customer. No thoughtful heart-to-heart. It was that night, standing on an empty, old brick street, looking up at the stars.

Our year had been filled with upheaval—a closed bookstore, a new job offer for Jordan, the departure of friends, uncertainty in our changing faith. Moving should have felt even more disruptive, but instead, I found myself breathing a sigh of relief. It was time to start over. We could plant new roots in this town. We could have a quiet sort of adventure.

We bought our first home, a little gray house close to our new downtown, with a front porch and a swing, just like I'd always wanted. I could walk to work when the humidity wasn't too suffocating, and we could see a school playground from our front door, hear the kids squealing and yelling and playing, the local high school marching band practicing before home football games. In the fall, our street was smothered and covered in trick-or-treaters, and in the summer, our old wooden door would swell shut. So much of life was familiar—we'd moved only forty-five minutes up the road—but we also felt like we'd entered a whole new world.

I sometimes have these extraordinarily realistic dreams when I sleep, where only a thing or two is "off," reminding me this isn't my real life but some fabrication of my imagination and psyche. Thomasville, at first, felt like one of those dreams. We were still in the South, still on a walkable tree-lined street, still living in an old, creaky house with some proximity to my parents, but things were different, too.

As we accepted various acquaintances' invitations to dinner, we learned about the countless acres of privately owned land surrounding Thomasville, used for fox and quail hunting. I'd only ever known people who fished or hunted deer, so when a man began unpacking the details of a local fox hunt, I blurted: "Oh! Like in *Mary Poppins*!" Everyone at the table laughed, but no one disagreed, and when Jordan was eventually asked to go dove hunting, I thought of Noah's dove in Genesis. I wondered aloud to Jordan if hunting an animal associated with peace was biblical, and we chuckled to ourselves, in private awe at all these things we didn't know. That first fall, I attended a gala for a local film festival at one of Ted Turner's estates (a completely ridiculous turn of phrase), and when I walked in, the living room was big and cavernous, the size of our entire home, with a taxidermic black bear standing on its hind legs next to a grand piano.

I felt, often, like Alice, accidentally down the rabbit hole.

For years, it felt like we'd moved, but we still weren't home. As usual, I turned to books for comfort and wisdom, reading *In Praise of Slowness* and *This Is Where You Belong*. We took long drives on the dirt roads winding around all that privately owned land, grateful for its preservation but also curious why we couldn't access any of it. We visited local museums and tried churches of every size, style, and denomination. One Sunday, we attended a contemporary service at the local Methodist church; all the worship leaders were in cowboy hats and boots, wearing jeans and playing banjos. *Is this just how people worship in South Georgia?* we wondered, until the very end of the service, when it was revealed we'd stumbled into their annual bluegrass Sunday.

Thomasville didn't feel like home, but that didn't change the reality that it *was*. So we finally stopped saying yes to things that didn't feel like us. I didn't attend any more galas; Jordan never hunted quail. Those things were fine, but they weren't what we'd done anywhere else, in any of our previous lives. Buying the bookstore hadn't changed who we were, so perhaps it was time to stop pretending it had.

There's this great Flannery O'Connor quote I love: "When in Rome, do as you done in Milledgeville." In other words, no matter where you go, take your home with you. Be who you were when you were most at home.

When we stopped pretending to be Thomasville, to be like the people who'd called her home for centuries, we finally could love her for ourselves. I took long, meandering walks down sidewalk-lined streets, through parks, in and around downtown. We sat on our porch steps and admired every pink-and-purple sunset. We ate meals at our favorite restaurants, walking to them when we could, overjoyed at the realities of living in a truly walkable town. We invited our faraway friends to come visit, so we could see our new home through their eyes. I swung in our porch swing and read book after book after book. We brought our lawn chairs out for nights at the amphitheater, attended every parade. I noticed cars would pull over for funeral processions, and I found myself doing the same. I joined a committee for the town's One Book celebration, where the whole city reads the same book together, and I bought season tickets for a local concert series. I said yes to selling books at special events at the country club, but we never joined the country club. I helped start a local organization for women entrepreneurs, and I attended downtown merchant meetings. We finally found a local church community and placed membership.

I cannot overemphasize how long all this took. I thought community could be built in months. Maybe, if the wheels turned really slowly, a year or two. But it took a decade. I was living somewhat in the shadow of the bookstore's previous owner. It wasn't her fault, nor was it mine. Thomasville had to get to know me, which meant I had to stop saying yes to the things she would have said yes to and instead had to begin saying yes to the things I knew fit me best. Do as you done in Milledgeville.

Jordan and I remained ourselves, but with our feet firmly planted in a town that, at first, didn't belong to either of us. In our first months there, a woman asked me if I was a local. "Oh yes!" I replied enthusiastically, relieved to be asked. "I'm originally from Tallahassee." She looked at me in pity, shaking her head. "Oh, honey. That's not local." Another well-intended customer asked for my last name. When I told her it was Jones, she asked which ones I was related to. I was confounded. Were there Joneses I should have been related to? (Yes.)

But in the middle of all this, there were pocket parks and a pizza place half a mile from our home. There were tall whispering pines, magnolia trees, and blooming roses on white picket fences. There were those pink-and-purple sunsets, a water tower and church steeple on the horizon. There were outdoor concerts and festivals, chill-inducing performances at the local cultural center two blocks down. There was the old gazebo next to the infamous Big Oak (ca. 1680) where I could sit and read, church bells chiming in the distance.

There were so many things to love.

A couple of years ago, after nearly a decade of living in Thomasville, I was asked by the city's tourism director if I could serve as a judge for the town's Rose Parade floats during our community's annual Rose Show and Festival. I'm not sure I'd ever been so honored in my life. On a beautiful spring day in April, I sat in a golf cart with my fellow judge, a man who's called Thomasville his home since childhood. We rode from float to float, making our comments in pencil on rustling sheets of paper. I felt like Maureen O'Hara in *Miracle on 34th Street*; the Macy's Thanksgiving Day Parade could not have been more thrilling to me.

After my judicial duties were complete, Jordan met me in the grandstand, where we watched the 101st Rose Parade from cold bleachers while the sun set in the distance and a breeze kept the humidity at bay. A street dance with a swing band immediately followed.

"I think you did it," Jordan said to me, smiling as the music played.

"Did what?" I asked.

"I think you made it in Thomasville."

It took ten years.

I'd thought when we bought the bookstore, that would be enough. Thomasville would love us for our commitment, and we, in return, would love her back.

That's not how it went. Small-town life was not the easy adjustment I thought it would be, and building community remains a constant work in progress. Life is not an episode of *Gilmore Girls*, and I am hardly Lorelai.

But I do love this town. When I sit in the darkened performing arts center, chills prickling my arms, I think how lucky I am to live here. When I walk my dog in the park and unlock the bookstore on a quiet weekday morning, I feel like I am living the dream. When I pull into my driveway and hear the cheers from the football game and see the sparkling stars in that vast black sky, I know I am home.

I didn't have to change who I was for this to be so. But I did have to learn to be comfortable in my own skin. I did have to realize there would always be pockets in this city where I wouldn't belong. We weren't made to fit everywhere. Wouldn't it be awful if we were?

I had to carve out my own place, and I think with time and practice and patience, I did.

CHAPTER 7

# On Being the Boss

A few years ago, while at a tea shop in London, I began to cry in front of a group of near strangers. We were talking about our businesses, our lives, and I'd mentioned how bossing felt a little like what I pictured mothering to be, how you train and shape your employees until they're prepared for something even better. "I know I've done my job well when someone leaves," I recall saying, somewhat proudly. How healthy! How mature! Then a pair of wise eyes looked at me from across the table and responded, "That sounds incredibly lonely. Who takes care of you while you stay?"

Cue the tears.

Retail is a field with notoriously high employee turnover. I did not know this when I took over the bookstore, because I had never worked retail before. Even my summer jobs in high school and college were in state government, where people regularly stay, some well past their expiration dates. I had no concept of retail life, no understanding of seasonal work.

Now, of course, I do. Over ten years of entrepreneurship has meant dozens of goodbyes. Hellos, too, but the goodbyes are harder, more memorable.

In the latter and waning days of the pandemic, I said goodbye to one of our bookstore employees who'd been with us for a couple of years. It was time; she had a move on the horizon, a growing family, and as a shop, we were in the middle of our own upheaval, trying to find a way forward after Covid. But it was still sad. Goodbyes, even when the timing is good and proper and well planned, can be gut-wrenching, and as much as I pride myself on preparing our employees for their future lives, I hate it when the good ones go. If it were up to me, they'd stay forever.

It's no longer in vogue to call your coworkers your family, many internet think pieces have assured me, and I respect that healthy boundary. Michael Scott, I pray, I am not. My family is my family; my friends are my friends. My personal and professional lives are better when those designations exist. But in a staff so small, the word *coworker* can feel unbearably sterile and inaccurate. Every time a staffer leaves, I'm not just saying goodbye to an employee; I'm saying goodbye to a fellow laborer, to someone who's been in the trenches with me, to someone who's trusted me and our store's mission with their talent and their time. It's a sort of grief we don't address very much, the letting go and wishing well of someone you really have admired and enjoyed working alongside.

There have been awful and awkward goodbyes, too, goodbyes I wish had gone better or more according to plan.

I was twenty-seven and a brand-new owner of the bookstore when I had to fire someone for the first time. I'd inherited the previous owner's team, and after months of trying to make it work, it very clearly wasn't. I searched the internet for tips and called my dad and asked our then minister to pray I might be gentle and compassionate, even when dealing a blow to someone who'd worked for the store for so many years. It was awful, as horrible as I'd imagined it to be, and I was completely ill-equipped. I wanted to vomit, before and after, and over ten years later, these types of conversations have never gotten any easier. They feel like failures, missteps that with better business acumen could have been prevented.

Because being a boss isn't really mothering at all. It is its own burden, and not every leaving has been what I hoped it would be.

Like with so many things in adulthood, I can feel like I didn't sign up for this.

When I took over the bookstore, no one explained to me I would be staying while, over the years, others left. I honestly believed—and still believe, to some extent—The Bookshelf would be one of many seasons in my life. I didn't imagine a decade of staying. My brain wouldn't let me think that far. On the handful of occasions I did picture running the shop into my twilight years, I always imagined a Kathleen Kelly existence, with loyal staffers Birdie and George and Christina by my side. (Yes, this is another

*You've Got Mail* reference.) In my mind, they all stayed and worked at The Shop Around the Corner, together, forever, amen.

But they didn't, did they? Not even within the confines of the movie's happy ending. George went to Fox Books. Christina began earning her master's degree. Birdie had a beautiful apartment and probably loved retirement, maybe even fell in love with another fascist dictator.

Kathleen, if you'll recall, was left to close up the shop alone.

So much of what I do at The Bookshelf is the very opposite of what my soul thought it wanted. My entire life I have been a proponent of deep, grounded relationships. I want a few friends who know me excruciatingly, painfully well; if I am yours, I want to be yours for life. It's why I still talk to Morgan, whom I met in the second grade, why I daily send voice messages to a dear friend I first encountered over a decade ago, why Rachel who's known me since I was seventeen also invited me to her babies' first birthdays. It's why I am married to the goofy kid who sat two seats down from me my very first day of college. I want to be friends forever.

It is not lost on me, then, that Bookshelf life is about hundreds of relationships, few of them rooted, perhaps none of them life-long. This reality doesn't make them shallow, though, not at all. They're seasonal, but sacred in their own ways. These relationships now make up much of my life and community, and it is odd, yet another way I am being softened and refined by my work. Customers grow up; older ones die. Employees head off for their next grand thing. I remain.

I have typed and retyped this essay over and over and over again, because there's a part to this story that doesn't quite fit the narrative I've written for myself. It is true: Retail is transient work with high turnover, and over the years I have said goodbye to dozens of employees, people I respected and still love.

But against all odds and industry norms, many of the current Bookshelf staffers are stayers. I am laughing as I type this, because almost every current shop employee has been with the store for a year or more. Two of them have been with me for half a decade, half of my Bookshelf tenure. Another one started as a store customer in high school and has literally grown up before my eyes. It's pretty remarkable, something I could not have predicted when I sat in that London tea shop. I assumed everyone would eventually leave, and I'd be the last one standing.

I still think it's a good thing to assume. I think it's good to hold relationships like these loosely, for staffers to have the freedom to leave when grad school or new jobs or significant others come calling. I want to be a person who means it when she says: "Of course! You should go!"

But I also want to be a person who is accepting of those who, like me, want to stay. I want The Bookshelf to be their safe landing place, a spot where their gifts and talents are used and appreciated and cultivated into something they can truly be proud of.

Their staying, of course, means they will inevitably see me make mistakes. This is the other part of bossing I don't see discussed in the business books I hate. The longer an employee spends at The Bookshelf, the more likely they are to see me stum-

ON BEING THE BOSS

ble, to witness my tears, my frustration, the occasional accidental expletive.

For so long, I thought being the boss meant being the best, most professional version of yourself. "Never let them see you sweat," etc. There are days when maybe that's true, when a staffer glances at me from across the room during an event, and I smile and act like we're totally prepared, even if we're not. But the longer I have a team who sticks around, the more comfortable I've become with the phrases "I'm sorry" and "I don't know" in regular and repeat circulation.

Watching employees leave is riddled with heartbreak, grief, maybe concern I haven't done enough. Watching employees stay is humbling, an acknowledgement they will see me at my worst, and I will see them at theirs, and we will choose to move forward, together.

I was on a walk one day, sharing all this with a friend who works in education. It can be easy to isolate myself, to act like no one outside of entrepreneurship understands the burden of bossing. I have learned this could not be further from the truth.

My friend spends her days in school, and every May, no matter what, there is graduation: hundreds of goodbyes. She commented how every year, some teachers seem truly sad, aware of the bittersweetness of the milestone, tearfully saying goodbye to the students who have been in their care. Others, she said, seem callous, removed, like they've stayed so long they no longer feel called to mourn when the year and those relationships all come to a close.

When I become callous to my employees' leaving or staying, it will be time for me to move on.

Until then, I'll be here. I will root for staffers and cheer for—I hope even prepare them for—their next steps. When and if our parting isn't what I pictured, I will still hope the best for them. I will say goodbye in sadness, and it will be genuine. I will mean it. I'll close up the shop and whisper gratitude for the role they played in keeping me here, in making this dream of mine come true. I will honor what we built together, and I'll keep it going because the work of their hands made it possible.

CHAPTER 8

# Obituaries

Running a small business in a small town is more googling of death notices than you might think.

The pandemic made us acutely aware of something experts now call "disenfranchised grief," a grief that doesn't fit societal norms, because the rise of online friendships and relationships means a lot of us wind up grieving people we might never have met in "real life."

I've experienced those losses, too, but I've yet to encounter a Reddit thread or a *New York Times* piece that could have prepared me for the losses of customers and how deep my grief for them might go. As with so many aspects of entrepreneurship, no one prepared me for this.

The more romantic side of small-business ownership—the part I pictured—is me, growing older and wiser year after year, bearing witness to the growing up of our youngest customers. The toddlers

I met during those first bookstore years are teenagers now, barely recognizable except for their sneaky, still-familiar grins or their penchant for good books or their willingness to accept brief greetings and hugs behind the register. I knew it would be a privilege to be the "book lady" for this small town, to be the person who read stories to a new baby or visited the local preschools. I longed to fill that type of communal role, saw the deep and lasting value in it and impact of it.

What I didn't understand is if you and your younger customers are growing up and older, your elderly customers are, too.

So, over the years, I've started to pay attention when someone doesn't come into the store with the frequency they once did. I grow worried over books left in the special-order bins for too long, pull our manager aside when I haven't seen someone in a while, turn to the internet as a last resort, dreading what Google results I might find, because no one calls their local bookseller when their mother passes away.

Instead, being a bookseller is what I imagine being a bartender must be like. The customers we encounter stand at the register and tell us about their lives, occasionally whispering as if in confession. Over the years, the conversations inevitably veer into the personal, and they become so much more than customers. They are, in a way, our friends. So our staff now begins to notice when a customer moves more slowly or grows more wrinkled. We are on high alert, because we understand we won't know when a visit to The Bookshelf might be someone's last. The store has made us so much more aware of this transitory life, the impermanence of it.

It is one thing to watch your parents grow older. You see them, if you're lucky, with more frequency. You're aware of their doctors' visits, their health history, their own parents' longevity.

There are occasions in which I have not even known a customer's last name.

A few weeks before the pandemic became the pandemic, Olivia, our store's operations manager, started to wonder about our friend Al. She couldn't get a hold of him for his special orders—a now telltale sign to us something is wrong—and he wasn't returning our calls. I wondered, too, but winter, even our mild version, can be hard for our older customers, and my internet searches offered no answer. Al was, we concluded, fine, but hunkered down at home until warmer weather prevailed. No news, we figured, was good news.

Days passed, and Olivia again asked about Al. I searched online, once again, to no avail, then tried Facebook. I wish I hadn't.

I wish I'd been alone when I made the discovery, wish I hadn't been halfheartedly looking for answers, assuming I'd find none, wish I wasn't some internet sleuth always digging around, wish I didn't have to look at my manager and give her the sad news no one wants to give. I wish especially I wasn't in my thirties, wish I wasn't a boss, wish I wasn't a person constantly expected to do and say hard things, so often unprepared.

Al was eighty-three years old when he died, and once I found his obituary, I agreed with every word. According to the writer, Al "thought of everyone he met as a friend." What a relief and comfort to know who he was in our store was who he was everywhere.

Look, Al certainly had his favorites (Olivia). But he loved all of us well, coming into the store after his workouts at the local gym, asking right when he walked in the door, "How are my girls?" in his still-heavy Staten Island accent. Al was a former salesman—a good one, no doubt—who frequently came in to hang out at his favorite downtown spot, offering kindness to women he treated like granddaughters. When our bookseller Nancy lost her husband, Al reached out in sympathy and understanding. He was a class act of the highest caliber. You know how I know?

Because I just work retail, and he treated me like royalty.

A lot of our older male customers are patronizing. (One infamously once asked to meet our owner, and when I introduced myself, he laughed and remarked, "They're letting eight-year-olds run bookstores now?") Some of them are sexist and short-tempered. Al looked me in the eye and asked how business was going. He complimented the store and our customer service. He knew every single one of our staffers by name. He talked to us at length, many times staying well past what any of us had time for, but even when we minded, we didn't really, if that makes any sense at all, because it was Al.

The funny thing is, as far as I could tell, Al wasn't a big reader. What Al did was purchase dozens of big band and jazz CDs. I special ordered them for him once, the day he came into the shop and introduced himself. He'd just moved to the area to be closer to his son, and if I could find him this CD he was looking for, he said he'd be my customer for life.

I did, and he was.

What do I say about someone who wasn't really mine, but who felt like it? What do I say about someone I knew but also didn't?

Al treated our bookstore staffers like granddaughters, but of course, someone else rightly called him "Granddad." We only saw him once every week or so, holding his CDs until he was ready, ordering the most obscure music you could possibly imagine, hearing snippets and stories of his life in pieces and parts. We caught only a glimpse of who Al was, but it was a memorable glimpse.

How I feel about Al is the same way I feel about Paula, a customer who ordered romance novels and brought us treats and one day surprised us with a small wooden painting of the store's exterior, cut from wood and done in intricate detail with the blues and greens the store is known for. I didn't even know she could paint. All we really knew about Paula was her love for mass-market paperbacks and that she wore scrubs. Now her painting hangs in my office, a reminder of who she was, at least to us.

It's not a lot to go on, but I really do believe you can know a lot about a person based on how they treat people, particularly people in service industries. Indie-bookstore workers can be high-minded, considering themselves party to a virtuous calling, like they're doing good and sacred and noble work. To be sure, I think we are. But also, we work retail. In the hierarchy of industry, we're rather low, and many of our customers treat us as such.

But other customers are like Paula, who chatted with us at the register and made us cookies and died too young.

I've been in enough therapy sessions to know my love and attention for our older customers has something to do with the loss of my grandparents. My grandmothers died right as Jordan and I were uprooting our lives, moving to Thomasville, and taking over the store. I grew up in small, multigenerational churches, and we'd just left that part of our life behind, too. I think I clung to any customer who vaguely reminded me of my grandparents, including Rose.

Rose had glorious white hair, curled and styled like my grandmother. She walked into the store one afternoon in a loose purple blazer and took my breath away, the picture of elegance and grace. I liked her from the moment I met her. She introduced herself to me with a sweet southern accent—the classy kind, the kind where your r's quietly disappear into nothing—and she was the first Thomasville customer who didn't seem automatically disappointed by my presence. In fact, she seemed delighted. She told me how glad she was I had taken over the store. At that point in time, no one, and I do mean no one, had told me that. I hardly knew how to respond to such a positive interaction.

Over the years, I realized Rose was a diverse and avid reader. It was almost a decade before I knew even a sliver of the whole story, that Rose had gotten her master's degree in English education, that she'd taught high school literature and English for years before moving to Thomasville in her retirement. I hadn't known, until I came across her obituary, that Rose had helped put her husband through seminary by working at Columbia University. I'd known she'd attended the local Methodist church, but I hadn't known she'd received the Quiet Disciple Award from her denomination.

I hadn't known those things, but I hadn't needed to, because they match entirely with the person I knew Rose to be. She showed me who she really was by loving me and respecting me, even though she knew me only a little, as her local bookseller.

If I am lucky and own The Bookshelf long enough, I will live through the deaths of countless Als and Paulas and Roses. And although I know such an outcome would be a privilege, the prospect makes me sad. It feels lonely, to keep loving people you don't really know, and depressing, to be forced to learn about their deaths through an internet search. I always believed my relationships would be deeper than this.

How naive, because the relationships that make life worth living are often the fleeting ones, the seasonal ones, the acquaintanceships we can't ever seem to define.

In our culture's current crisis of loneliness, the answer, experts say, isn't to form more deep and lasting friendships. It's to stop using the self-checkout at Target. It's to stop placing a mobile order for your coffee. It's to look people in the eye and to make purchases in person and to form the societal bonds we've almost forgotten out of a desire for convenience.

Indie bookstores are, by their very existence, inconvenient. You have to order your mass-market romance novels and wait to pick them up instead of downloading them instantly to your Kindle. But I never would have met Paula if she'd just read her books on an e-reader. Al could have easily and more inexpensively, I'm sure, ordered his CDs from eBay or Amazon. But because he chose inconvenience, I will remember Al and his kindness until I, too, turn to dust.

When I first wrote about Al in a newsletter after his death, one of my online friends reached out. "This reminds me of a recent thing I read about the virtue of affability," she said. "It sounds like Al personified affability."

I'd never heard affability described as a virtue in the way this commenter meant, but apparently, in the Catholic Church (and in classical philosophy, thank you, Aristotle), there are four cardinal virtues: prudence, justice, fortitude, and temperance. Other virtues are filed under those "big four" (my term, not Aristotle's), and the virtue of affability is considered a virtue under justice. It is, simply put, the virtue of approachableness. According to the *Modern Catholic Dictionary*, affability "partakes of justice in that a person adjusts to other people, giving each one the respect he or she deserves."

It is the virtue, I think, of the holy fool, the virtue we see displayed in Ted Lasso as he befriends and listens to everyone he meets. It is undoubtedly the virtue I saw displayed in Al, and in Paula, and in Rose. It is the virtue that just might have the power to cure our collective loneliness. It is the virtue I hope is displayed in me, as I stand behind a counter and offer smiles to the customers whose last names I may never know.

# CHAPTER 9

# Sally Field Syndrome

I found this sentence, tucked in an email draft I suppose I was using as my journal one day, circa 2021: "The Bookshelf has taken on a life of its own these last few months, and words can't describe my excitement and, somehow, simultaneously, my horror."

You'd think I would have been ecstatic. Not only did our store survive a pandemic, but she grew. Thanks to marketing efforts like our store podcast and Instagram account, we were able to pivot relatively quickly back in March 2020, earning new-to-us long-distance customers who kept us afloat through their purchases and support. During those early pandemic days, our store manager and I went to The Bookshelf every day to package and ship orders to readers all over the country, even when it felt like the world was ending. I'd always wondered what type of person I'd be during the apocalypse, and the answer, I'm sad to have discovered, is I'd just work through it. I'd just keep doing my normal, everyday tasks in the assumption things would eventually reach equilibrium. (I don't love this about myself.)

So we gained all these wonderful new customers. People called us on the phone, kept us company, ordered puzzles when their families got bored from the together time the pandemic required.

I was relieved. I still carry in my shoulders the stress and the weight of those years. Every day, I wondered if it would be our last day. Every day, I wondered if we'd make enough money to pay our team. Every day, I wondered what the point of it all was.

A lot of small businesses closed during the pandemic, and although I have no doubt owners made those decisions based on finances and a disrupted world, I also wonder if they were just tired. Pivoting was exhausting, decision-making even more so. I want to say I was crippled by decision fatigue, but I couldn't *not* make decisions. That wasn't an option; people were counting on me. I just kept putting one foot in front of the other, and all these years later, it's still a stress-filled blur.

When vaccines rolled out, and life returned to some semblance of its prepandemic glory, we retained a lot of those found-us-during-Covid customers. Our podcast listenership grew, and, again, so did the number of Instagram followers. The numbers were big, not viral big (nightmare), but big for our small town, and for me.

I'd purchased The Bookshelf in 2018 because I'd envisioned a quiet life for me and for Jordan, working and living in a small southern town, like Father Tim in Jan Karon's Mitford series, like the Bible verse I'd loved and memorized in childhood: "Make it your ambition to lead a quiet life: You should mind your own business and work with your hands."

Were you living a quiet life if thirty-five thousand people were following your business on Instagram? When we reached the milestone of three million downloads for our podcast (unfathomable to me), I felt like throwing up. Millions of people had listened to my voice, and guess what? They didn't all like what they heard.

It's difficult for me to envision watching a TV show or listening to five hundred episodes of a podcast, all while not liking the characters or the voice of the host, but I quickly discovered—thanks to an inbox full of emails and anonymous DMs and flippant Instagram comments and Apple Podcasts reviews—lots of people could.

People didn't like my voice and thought I giggled too much. They preferred our male guests and cohosts. They didn't like how I ended many of my sentences with "Right?" They were specific and somehow also nebulous in their critiques, and although years of retail work had curtailed my people-pleasing tendencies, they were still there, lying dormant, only to be awoken by an email from a listener asking me not to have one cohost or another on the show anymore.

For a couple of years, when these voices were the loudest, I wore a necklace Jordan gave me with the words "IN THE ARENA" stamped in almost imperceptible print across a tiny gold bar. I'd borrowed the words from President Theodore Roosevelt's famous "Man in the Arena" speech: "It is not the critic who counts; not the man who points out how the strong man stumbles, or where the doer of deeds could have done them better. The credit belongs to the man who is actually in the arena, whose face is marred by dust and sweat and blood; who strives valiantly; who errs, who comes short again and again . . ."

I'd repeat some portion of those words to myself every time I read a negative review or intercepted a cruel phone call or overheard an unkind word about the store. I loved The Bookshelf, and to stay devoted to her would require thicker skin than I possessed. I'd always envisioned myself as strong and unfazed, unaffected by the opinions of others, but with The Bookshelf, I perhaps incorrectly believed opinions affected sales. I worried one wrong move, one misstep, would send me and the store into bankruptcy, would bring pain and unemployment to the members of our staff. I didn't think I had to be perfect, but I thought I had to be close. At the very least, I needed to be likable, to be the Sally Field of Thomasville, beloved by her peers and lauded with surprising praise. Sally Field, I thought, could lead a store through the pandemic and come out on the other side with her optimism still intact. Mine, though, was missing in action.

Of course, it wasn't just the pandemic, and it wasn't just comments from random strangers on the internet. I started going to therapy back in 2017. This was before it felt like therapy was everywhere; a couple of my friends were counselors and therapists, and after four years of running The Bookshelf, I thought it might be beneficial to talk with an unbiased, neutral professional. And although I now cover all sorts of topics in therapy, both personal and professional, for years all I talked about was The Bookshelf.

I talked about employees and being a boss and how terrifying it all was. I talked about letting people down and disappointing people and the immense pressure I felt I was under. I talked about the woman who told me, to my face, she thought I was a fake entrepreneur, the man who teased that a child was running The Bookshelf. I talked about these things while sitting on a couch and making jokes and occasionally sniffling into a tissue because I did not know where else to go. I did not know where to take these things. I knew I could talk to Jordan, to my parents, and I did, but they weren't neutral. Jordan is about as unbiased a spouse as they come, but I still needed someone who didn't love me to tell me these voices didn't matter.

When you run a business for more than a decade, there are countless times you think you'll quit. When we got our first tax bill—I naively thought we'd get a refund, like we did in our pre-entrepreneurship days—we owed so much money I thought I'd faint in the accountants' office. I wanted to quit. When I was waiting to board a plane in the Baltimore airport, reading some of the most awful Instagram comments I'd ever seen, I burst into tears and started pacing at an empty gate. I thought my career was over. I wanted to quit. When a woman's cruel words made me cry on the floor of The Bookshelf's bathroom, I wanted to quit. When a Thomasville native told me I wasn't local and would never belong, I wanted to quit. When a former staffer tweeted how he felt about me as a boss, I wanted to quit. When the local bank wouldn't give me a small loan to make it through Christmas, I wanted to quit. When my favorite staffers over the years have graciously moved on, I've wanted to quit with them.

But I stay. A lot of the time, I'm not even sure why or how.

Therapy helps. Learning which voices matter helps. (Setting aside money for taxes every year also helps.)

For a couple of years, I met every month or so with a group of women to talk about business. I couldn't believe these smart, wise women were encountering some of the same entrepreneurial problems I found plaguing me. They, too, struggled with taxes and customer service and never-ending feedback. I think it was my friend Ruth Ann who mentioned the concept of a board of directors. The Bookshelf doesn't have a literal board of directors, but she encouraged me to think about who would be on my metaphorical one. "If they're not on your board of directors," she said, "they don't get a vote. They don't get a voice."

This changed my life.

I no longer read reviews, positive or negative. I rarely read the comments on The Bookshelf's Instagram account, though they've gotten better over time. When our podcast was in a transition period, and the comments seemed unusually aggressive and loud, my then business coach told me, firmly, not to respond. To do my best to tune those words and those voices out. I did, and I think ignoring them took away some of their power. We still get the occasional rude DM, but it's rarely to the extreme it once was. I hope we've cultivated a culture where people know those words won't be given weight here. They don't matter, so they're not worth your breath or the time it takes you to tap them out on your phone.

On my personal Instagram accounts, I've set "trigger words" Meta prevents me from seeing. I block or delete people who are merciless or who are hateful or whom I don't know. As Taylor sings, "This is our place. We make the rules."

This doesn't mean I avoid criticism. I simply want to listen to the voices of those who are invested and who matter, the people who know The Bookshelf and me well. I pay attention to people I'm in actual relationship with, and I listen to the feedback from customers who I know financially support the store. When there are criticisms about what books we stock or which authors we host or whose voices come on the podcast, I listen with curiosity, and I take note of trends. Sometimes that feedback results in changed business practices; sometimes it doesn't. I trust my staff, my husband, my family, my friends, and my community.

When we hosted a party to celebrate ten years of owning and running The Bookshelf, Jordan gave a toast. There were probably seventy or so people in the room, and Jordan told them: "Annie and I talk a lot about what voices matter in the running of The Bookshelf. You are the voices who matter." They were customers who'd been kind to me instantly, or who'd eventually trusted me with this town's bookstore. They were our staffers, former and current. They were my family, my priest, one of my best friends from childhood. They were people who I knew loved the store, and they also loved me.

I am going to make mistakes. I am going to say things I shouldn't, and despite my best efforts, I am going to misstep in my life and in the life of the store. Love tells us, gently, when we're wrong. I'll listen to the voice of love.

But I won't listen to emails or comments or critiques by people who do not have my best interest at heart. There's not enough time, and I don't have thick enough skin for it. I just don't.

I can keep running The Bookshelf only if I hold close to the people whose voices matter most. I stay, not because I am Sally Field, likable and adorable, but because I am in therapy. I have a business coach. I have friends and family who love and support me, and not because of what I do for The Bookshelf. I have a faith that grounds and cements me, so staying is doable because The Bookshelf is only one small part of who I am. I guess if that makes me a fake entrepreneur or too giggly to take my job seriously, guilty as charged.

I've admittedly always gotten a kick out of that Sally Field moment when she stands at the Oscars podium and proclaims, with tears in her eyes and arms spread wide, "You like me! Right now. You like me!"

But I don't feel that way. I never have, but especially not since The Bookshelf entered my life. Instead, I feel immense thanks and relief when I type, with tears in my eyes and humor in my heart: You don't have to like me. You really don't have to like me. I promise I'll be okay.

# PART III

# Staying Faithful

*Gradually I remembered what I had known all along, which is that church is not a stopping place but a starting place for discerning God's presence in this world.*

—Barbara Brown Taylor, *Leaving Church*

# CHAPTER 10

# When Staying True Means Leaving

This does not feel like a deconstruction story. I wish it were, because, looking back, if I could have named it something, it might have helped. But in 2012, we weren't talking about deconstruction. We were just falling apart.

I was born the daughter and granddaughter of faith-filled people. At the peak of my childhood, my family took up two pews in a dark brown wood-paneled church, where each Sunday, they'd lift their voices in four-harmonied praise. I'd watch as my parents and grandparents, aunts and uncles, drank grape juice silently and soberly from tiny plastic cups. I wondered when it would be my turn, when I'd walk out of the family pew and down the aisle and toward the baptistry, where I'd put on a white robe, and then Christ, and be forever changed.

Faith in God was not hard for me as a child. It was the air I breathed, and everyone I knew breathed it, too.

The specifics, though, could get tricky. When I was in the second grade, I began attending a Baptist school in our town, and I remember my third grade teacher asking me if I was saved. *Saved from what*? I wondered, but soon I learned: this was another language of the Christian faith, and it was one I didn't know. I'd gone to church my whole life, but here my teachers and peers saw God differently, talked about him differently. I thought I knew the language, but I didn't.

I was twelve, inching closer to what our church considered the "age of accountability." I hadn't made that walk toward the baptistry yet, hadn't been immersed under those miraculous waters. So when my sixth grade teacher made us bow our heads and close our eyes during class one day, and she asked the same question I'd heard at least once a year since the second grade ("Have you asked Jesus into your heart?"), I deviated from my usual response. I said no. It felt like the most honest answer I could give. Then my teacher asked me to stay after school, and I guess she would have saved me then and there had my mother not come in and saved me first.

My mother doesn't get angry often, but that day, she was furious. She believed in a child's innocence, and she did not believe in indoctrination, so she raged at my poor teacher, who I now know was just trying to keep one of her young students from the gates of hell.

This was when the questions started getting louder. I couldn't reconcile the truths I was hearing at church from the different-but-similar truths I was hearing at school. I went to my most trusted adviser, my grandfather, and we began reading the Bible together, because he assured me the Bible had any answer I would ever need, and that as a preteen, I was entirely capable of studying and learning and knowing everything there was to know about God and faith and humanity. I was smart and studious, and the Word of God had all the answers, and supposedly, none of the confusion. (I did not find this to be the case.)

My grandfather died the first week of my seventh grade year. I had just memorized my locker combination. I don't remember now if we'd even finished reading the Bible together, but I do know he died in August, and I got baptized the following May, because I didn't want to never see him again. I was old enough, according to my church, to know the difference between right and wrong, so the longer I waited to be baptized, the closer I was to an eternity away from all the people I loved.

I thought baptism, like the Bible, would solve my problems, quiet my questions. I thought the Holy Spirit would feel like something, maybe bring me peace or assurance or certainty. But no matter how many times I read the Bible in its entirety, no matter my Sunday-morning baptism, the questions continued. I'd attend Fellowship of Christian Athletes meetings at my school on Friday mornings, smiling and singing to a guitar-led praise band, then attempt to sing alto on Sunday mornings, sans even a piano, because the worship I'd done on Friday I was told was false compared to the worship I'd engage in on Sunday. Singing and making melody in your heart did *not* include instrumentation.

At my school, I'd lead devotionals and watched female students and teachers speak in chapel services. I'd pray aloud in a mixed group of my peers. At my church, women taught Sunday school until the boys turned thirteen and were baptized. Then those little boys were taught by men, because women couldn't hold leadership positions or usurp authority from men, and those boys were now, somehow, men. The women I saw on Sundays and Wednesdays didn't preach or teach or pray, except they did in my home and in our car and at our table, because my mother prayed all the time, everywhere. Even the church couldn't prevent me from my mother's witness.

My church taught me that my school's teachings were wrong. There was only one way to follow Jesus, and we knew exactly what it was because we read the Bible.

This was confusing to me, because all my teachers and friends also read their Bibles, but their interpretations were occasionally different from ours. How could I believe or serve a God who would punish faithful people for trying?

By the time I graduated high school, I was ready for a more seamless Christian existence. I was exhausted from spiritual whiplash, and I applied only to Church of Christ colleges, a decision I never questioned. I wanted to go to school with people who interpreted the Bible like I did. I wanted my questions to be answered, or better yet, ended. Finished. No more.

Instead, I carried my adopted evangelicalism with me. I couldn't shake it. After years spent befriending people in other denominations, I was not Church of Christ enough for this very southern Church of Christ school. The first time I sat down at a cafeteria table, the guys seated around me played a game to see who would have to say the blessing over the food. Everyone rushed to put up a thumb, and the last person to lift a thumb would be forced to pray. I'd never seen this game (it's not a very good one), so I didn't put up a thumb. I shrugged. "I'll pray," I said. The guy across from me, who'd eventually become a dear friend, quickly intervened. "No, I've got it!" he insisted. I was confused, until I realized he'd really protected me. Not everyone at the table was comfortable with a woman praying in front of men.

My junior year, when our college president shut down student-led devotionals that were using instrumental praise music, I was enraged. I was also the editor of the student paper, and I knew what a pen had the power to do. I wrote scathing editorials and investigative feature stories that eventually led me to the president's office, where I sat alone while an old man with white hair accused me over and over again of not speaking the truth in love.

Still, I stayed. I didn't know how not to. Everyone in my life stayed. My parents stayed, despite their own hurts and ostracism. Until adulthood, I never heard them complain. They had questions, too, but when my brother and I brought ours to the dinner table, my parents just listened. I think we were learning together, and it was easier to stay, to try to make small differences wherever and however we could.

It's how I wound up teaching Sunday school to teenage girls after I graduated college. I was back home at the same church I'd attended in childhood. My family was still there, and it all felt comfortable at first, like putting on a pair of comfy sweatpants, until suddenly you realize the elastic is worn out, and those pants don't quite fit like they used to.

But anybody can make a pair of sweatpants last forever, and that's what I intended to do. I would attend church there forever, and I'd quietly subvert the teachings I believed were false. I'd empower little girls and raise questions in our small groups, and I'd make the church better by staying.

It all came crumbling down, of course. It always does. A mother didn't like what I'd taught her teenage daughter during a Wednesday-night class (I'd said we all go through spiritual deserts at some point in our lives), and there was poor church leadership, no oversight, no real system, and despite women being so often told to be silent, this wealthy woman's voice was heard. I was no longer allowed to teach; I could coteach with Jordan, but even that became suspect. Church elders wondered if I spoke too much in those sessions, commandeering my husband's authority.

I'd never intended to be a rabble-rouser or a troublemaker, but the questions that quietly plagued me in my adolescence now screamed. I began reading the prayer books of Phyllis Tickle, and I found comfort in the rhythms of liturgy. I read *Leaving Church* by Barbara Brown Taylor, and I felt so seen and known and understood, and all of a sudden I knew: staying isn't everything. "I wanted to recover the kind of faith that has nothing to do with being sure what I believe," wrote Taylor, "and everything to do with trusting God to catch me though I am not sure of anything." Me, too, I thought, almost desperately. Me, too.

We stuck around, though, for a long time. I went to church

with stomachaches and headaches. Our best friends, one by one, moved away. My parents didn't have comfort to offer; they were hurting and confused, too. Their foundation was slipping.

So when Jordan and I moved to a nearby small town, we left our church. I think everyone guessed we'd find a Church of Christ in our new town, and I liked the freedom that assumption offered us. Leaving church means different things to different people, to different denominations. Leaving our church meant renouncing our faith, losing our friends, separating ourselves from our families. Any respect we'd had or earned was lost. It was awful, lonely, painful. We both had disappointed people, so we clung to each other even when we didn't agree on a church we'd visited or why another wasn't a good fit.

I kept reading books, felt a part of me awaken when I encountered *Searching for Sunday* by Rachel Held Evans. Every week, Jordan and I would visit a different church, a different denomination, and every week, I'd cry. Cry because starting over is hard. Cry because we didn't fit anywhere. Cry because no one understood the leap we'd just made. Cry because I didn't know what was "right" anymore. Cry because I missed sitting by my parents, missed knowing every word to every song, missed the people who raised me, missed the simplicity of four-part harmony and grape juice in plastic cups.

We landed, for a while, at an Anglican cathedral. They had classes and resources to help answer our questions, but also they let our questions just . . . sit. Questions weren't disrespectful or threatening or scary, nor did they automatically come with black-and-white answers. Questions were just questions. Everybody had them. It was part of a life of faith.

I found that ambiguity odd but immensely comforting, and the church's openness—literal and metaphorical—even more so. Every Sunday, when the lector led the congregation in the Prayers of the People, he (or she!) would pray for other area churches of various denominations, by name. For someone who grew up being taught that everyone else was wrong, this prayer was revolutionary. I couldn't get over it. It widened the church for me, in some ways de-Americanized it. The church was big. God was big. I felt myself expanding. I could breathe again.

Sundays were not perfect, but nor were they stifling.

There are more stories to tell. Stories of the friendships we lost. Stories about the cathedral where we found God again, only to have it all turned upside down when the rector was disciplined and defrocked for severe wrongdoing. Stories of tracts in our mailbox and text threads about infant baptism and all the questions our families asked that we couldn't ever seem to answer correctly.

My parents eventually left our old church denomination. Our best friends did, too. I don't know if it's our fault or not. I was given a legacy of staying, and I worry, sometimes, that I threw that legacy away. But I'm more worried if I'd stayed, I might have lost my faith entirely. I'm worried the questions and, really, the answers would have eaten me alive. I'm worried I would have raised my children with the same wounds I had, and when they came to me battered, I wouldn't know how to help.

So I left. I left for myself, and for Jordan, and for our future. I left so I could stay close to Jesus, and I no longer believe I traded my inheritance for soup. I believe I now cling to something bigger, something less reliant on my own literal interpretation of a complicated book. My faith is messy and muddled and not at all certain or sure. There is fear and trembling at every turn. All these years later, and the wounds haven't quite scabbed over. I have plenty of bruises and scars, and occasionally, I bump against one and feel the ache. But God is still there, and he is big, so much bigger than the wood-paneled church told me he was.

For a while, I loved it there. It was, in its own way, easy. It is scary, a little lonely, in the wildernesses of our faith. But I breathe a little easier, too. The sky is wider out here. My legacy is different from the one my parents and grandparents gave to me, but I hope it is equally brave. I hope it is faithful. I hope it is good and deep and wide, with room to wrestle and grow and change.

Sometimes, to stay, you have to leave. It might be the best, hardest thing you ever do.

# CHAPTER 11

# Sharing a Pew & Passing the Peace

I love the quiet of an empty church building. If I could, I think I would spend hours soaking up the silence through wooden pews and cold marble floors. When Jordan and I travel, we visit all manner of houses of worship together, many of them ornate but peace-filled cathedrals. Jordan explores the art and the icons, and I do, too, but what I really want to do is sit. Maybe take a nap. Maybe listen to a choir practice or a pianist play. I'm in awe of the vastness of a cathedral, the smallness I feel in one, and there are so few places now where one can sit uninterrupted in silence.

How funny, then, that on Sunday mornings, when church buildings are presumably at their very best, filled to the brim with worshippers and incense and songs of praise, I feel adrift, unmoored, desperate to curl up in a ball and stay in bed. I don't find quite as much comfort in churches when they are doing what they were actually designed to do, and I find this disconcerting and potentially a little sinful.

Why would I rather sneak quietly into a cathedral on a Monday morning than enter with fellow believers on a Sunday? What does this say about me?

Although I'm not as pained by church services as I once was, I never wake up on a Sunday morning and think: *Yay! Hooray for what I get to do today!* That reality breaks my heart, but I'm coming to understand that my reluctance is understood and seen by my Creator. And even with my hesitance, Sunday mornings give me the gift of Communion, of Eucharist, of Sacrament, and even when my heart is hard, it softens at the sight of old men and little girls walking up the aisle to kneel at the foot of the cross.

Sundays, then, like so much else, are a mixed bag. I know this. I've come to accept it.

In the early days of our small-town existence, Jordan and I drove up to our church on a spring Sunday morning. I tilted my head toward the sun streaming through our car window, toward the blue sky, and I thought: *Today could be a good day.*

As we parked our car, I spotted the family of a woman whose position I'd recently had to change at the bookstore. After weeks of agonizing decision-making, I'd offered her a new role with different responsibilities and shorter hours. I did it in the kindest way I knew how, but adulthood has taught me that even when your intentions are pure and good and thoughtful and kind, they can be cruel to whoever is on the receiving end. I hate this piece of adulthood with every fiber of my being. I want good intentions to equal good results, good relationships, good in general. But they don't, not always, probably rarely.

So this staffer and I had experienced a slight fracture in our relationship. I'd lost her trust; her estimation of me had dropped significantly, noticeably, and we were, somehow, still going to church together, both trying desperately to pass the peace in the truest, deepest sense of the phrase.

When I saw her family, I felt a pang in my gut. I knew I had dropped in their estimation, too, knew I'd caused hurt even though my decisions were, I hoped, the best for the store, the best for the staffer, the best for me.

I took deep breaths as we parked our car, and I thought of that scene in *The Family Stone*, when Diane Keaton throws a fork at her son. He's been humiliated at the dinner table, and he's lost in his thoughts, and he's deaf. Throughout the movie, the family signs to him, and in this scene, his mother throws a fork at him to get his attention. She signs to him and tells him she loves him, she sees him, she understands him. He is hers.

Whenever I get bogged down in the hurts and pains of church—and there are so many, all these years into my spiritual journey—I think about God. I know church is other people, and I know a huge, large, vast part of the Christian life is to walk in step with other people. I know this, and it is hard, because people are hard. But I find comfort in a God who sees me, who will throw forks at me to get my attention. Church is community, but it's also about me and God.

I walked into church that spring morning, trying to focus on the me-and-God aspect of a Sunday. I walked through the doors and smack-dab into this staffer's family. Jordan and I had not stayed in the car long enough, and now we were face to face with people whom I knew I had hurt. But I smiled, and I tried to make eye contact without being aggressive about it. I tried to be demure and polite but not over-the-top, because I knew I'd caused pain, despite my best efforts, and nothing I could do, no smile I could offer, would ever be a big enough peace offering.

I received only an expressionless silence in return.

Hurt, I walked hurriedly, angrily, through the foyer of the church building, ignoring the glances of friends and fellow church-goers, until I reached the back door, walked out in tears, back to our car, and left. The sanctuary would hold no sanctuary for me that Sunday.

I once heard an interview Krista Tippett did with theologian Eugene Peterson. She asked him about his experiences within the Christian church, and Peterson shared how people would often come to him asking how to pick a church, what advice he had for pilgrims searching for home. I understand their question. At the time, Peterson was one of our greatest living theologians, and there's a huge swath of us, I think, wondering, *To whom shall we go?* forgetting, maybe, that the question has already been answered.

Anyway, Peterson responded to those searching people simply and surprisingly. "Go to the closest church where you live, and the smallest." Jordan and I were in the car listening to the interview together, and we looked at each other and smiled. We'd unintentionally done just that. We'd moved to a small town, and now we were attending the smallest church either of us had ever been a part of. (We were not particularly good at it, if you must know.)

And because I chose a small church in a small town, I now sit in pews—or near pews—of people who I know might not like me. I have to offer peace to customers who may have been rude to my employees, who may have been rude to me, who have, hopefully unintentionally, betrayed the call of Christ. Chances are high I've done something to hurt them, too.

It is all so fraught, kneeling and worshipping beside each other, broken.

I hate going to church alongside people who may not know me, love me, or understand me. Church, I was taught, should be a place you feel known and seen and loved, not belittled or hurt, judged or ignored.

But even as I type that, I know it's not true. My parents taught me to love church, to seek solace and peace in it, but I watched for years as they were overlooked, hurt, and treated poorly. They tried to hide their negative experiences, but I saw them. (I'm an eldest daughter; of course I saw them.) And I experienced my own church hurts, even as a little girl, especially in my teen years and into my early adulthood.

So no, a full Sunday-morning church building doesn't always signify peace or belonging to me. And Christ is where two or more

SHARING A PEW & PASSING THE PEACE

are gathered, yes, but his spirit is also in me every day, in every quiet moment, as I sit in my office, as I lie on the floor and stare at the ceiling, as I walk around my neighborhood and breathe in fresh air. God is above all and through all and in all, so it is not sinful to hear him most clearly in the quiet, with the rush of people and feelings and emotions taken away. If this is true for me, it is because he made me this way.

I hate recalling that Sunday morning. Back then, I hated the embarrassment of my tears. It brought me back to the younger version of myself, the young woman who got stomachaches every time she parked her car in the church parking lot.

But I'm also proud of the adult version of myself who knew: Nope. This is too much. I can smile and offer peace, and I can also remove myself, go to a place that feels safe, seek comfort in the quiet, find God where he is most easily knowable to me.

I do not want to be driven out of church by disappointment or hurt. Jesus means too much to me. I also know myself better than ever before, and I now take the appropriate steps to protect myself, and to create peace for my own heart and for the hearts of others. I remember the spaces where God speaks to me best, and I take deep breaths and try desperately to find him there.

And perhaps inexplicably, I keep going to a small church in my small town.

It's been many, many years since that interaction in the foyer of the church building, and there were passing moments I considered leaving altogether. There was, for me, a precedent for leaving; I thought it might be easier, and—quite frankly—I am an awkward person, and mostly what I want to do in church is sit on the back pew and quietly observe (and also make a quick exit). It would have been easy to leave.

But time, occasionally, does heal wounds. I don't know if a restored relationship ever looks exactly the way people expect it to look, but I do believe peace is possible, and over time, the staffer? I think she forgave me. And if she didn't, she managed to make peace with me. We'd smile at each other in the halls of our church building, tentative and tender. Peace doesn't always look, fully, like reconciliation. It's a little more akin to acceptance, an acknowledgement we're going to be okay with time. We began to make eye contact again, before Communion, or on my way back to the pew from my spot at the railing.

This is one of the things about liturgical worship that astounds me. In my childhood denomination, the church of my family of origin, Communion is brought to you in your pew, passed from person to person. It is silent, sober, and reflective, yes, but above all, it is deeply, deeply personal. Communion—despite what its name might have been intended to suggest—was between me and God. I would pray, and I would read my Bible, and I wouldn't make eye contact or a sound. In more liturgical worship services, Communion is *communal*. Families get up together; there's singing and fidgety children and movement between pews. There is no going unnoticed during Communion, and it's not as terrifying as it sounds. In fact, I wonder if the point is to witness one another in our humanness, to awkwardly cross over pews together, to squeeze in at a railing and kneel and offer up our hands as if it were something we do every day.

Before Communion, too, there is a moment, a time when the priest blesses the congregation, calling out, "Peace be with you," to which parishioners respond, "And also with you." We hug our spouses and our children, shake hands with people seated in front of or behind us, toss out peace signs to folks across the aisle. It's more than some kind of cheesy meet-and-greet with fellow believers; it's designed to ensure you're at peace with those around you. It's a moment requiring physical touch and bodily action. Peace, even when you might disagree. Peace, even when your relationship might not be perfect. Peace, even when your heart is in tumult. Peace, as preparation.

The acts of Communion and passing the peace saved my relationship with this woman.

Eventually, she moved from our community, found a job elsewhere. But before she left town, she came by my office, a brave act of grace. She thanked me for our time together, and I wished her well. I meant it.

My heart broke a little, because I knew I'd disappointed her. I'd delivered a professional setback, and I hated it. She was my sister in Christ, and I'd let her down.

But for months, we kept taking Communion together. We slowly made eye contact when passing the peace. We couldn't avoid each other, not in our small town, not in our small church.

And maybe that's the point. Relationships won't be mended

perfectly, but maybe with time and constantly running into one another at coffee shops, we'll be reminded we are all human. We all make mistakes. We are all—and I mostly believe this—trying our best.

I still think I did the best I could with that situation. Maybe somewhere, she's reading this, and thinking the same thing for her. Or maybe she hates me.

Either way: Peace be with you. And also with you. And also with me. We are doing our best.

# CHAPTER 12

# Lowering the Bar

Jordan once commented to me he thought true and lasting happiness could be found by lowering our expectations. Initially, this observation filled me with righteous indignation. By nature, I am a high-expectations person. I expect a lot of my spouse (sorry, Jordan!), my friends, my family, my institutions. Don't worry: I also expect a lot of myself. The very high bar I hold people to? I hold myself to it, too.

I want a lot out of life, and I worried if we lived by Jordan's lower expectations, we'd be sad, disappointed, glass-half-empty, always-expecting-the-worst kind of people.

When Jordan and I met back in college, we had a professor who asked each class member to evaluate their own happiness on a scale from one to ten: one, of course, being unhappy, and ten being the happiest you could possibly be. I proudly gave myself a ten, which I now know was insane. (As an aside, I'm an elder millennial, and we can learn a lot about elder millennials by the AIM screen names they gave themselves. Mine was hapygirl04, a name taken from the title of my then favorite Martina McBride song, "Happy Girl." I have always been a little obsessed with happiness and the happy life.)

Jordan, if I remember correctly, gave himself a six on the happiness scale, and I was devastated. Was I falling in love with an unhappy person? How could anyone dating me, a ten on the happiness scale, possibly be a six? What could we do to fix this? How could I help Jordan become his happiest self?

It should be noted Jordan wasn't concerned at all. When I asked him why he was so unhappy, he shrugged. "I'm not," he said. "But you're a six!" I recall shouting. "A six when you could be a ten!" He looked at me like I'd lost my mind, and maybe I had. "I think most people are probably around a six," he said calmly, "if they're lucky."

We've joked about this for years, my insistence on increasing Jordan's happiness, taking his entirely adequate level of happiness as my own personal mission.

It took adulthood for me to realize how right Jordan was, how life is rarely spent at the apex of happiness, but in the averages, the middles, the "just okays."

Which brings me, oddly, back to faith.

After we left the church denomination of our childhoods, we felt a little lost, unfocused, meandering. It was hard to find a new faith home, and perhaps the ironic thing about high expectations and high-happiness levels is you take those same assumptions into your institutions, too. As a result, I was an extremely critical churchgoer, even before we left our church of origin. After? I was on high alert for false teachings, inauthentic leaders, theologically unsound music selections, even grammatical errors in bulletins. I was on the hunt for unnecessary patriotism, for hypocrisy, for inaction toward injustice.

On my more wrongheaded days, I considered myself a hero. *The church needs people like me!* I would think to myself, upon rolling my eyes through one sermon or another. *Our generation needs truth-telling prophets*, I'd think, as if spotting a missing period in a PowerPoint presentation made me a modern-day Jeremiah.

The truth is that over the years, the critical thinking I prided myself on slowly turned me into a cynic, and it's pretty hard to believe in things like miraculous resurrection when you're consumed by your own cynicism. Faith and cynicism are not natural bedfellows.

It's also worth noting that, when put to the test, my critical prophet's eye didn't actually result in any positive change or revelation. The church we finally selected after months of searching was a large cathedral with rarely a misstep in music selection, with mostly sound theological teaching. Everything seemed to be done with professionalism and excellence. I was so grateful, finally, to have a place where I could shut down the voices in my head.

Then, a few years into our attendance there, the rector was found guilty of sexual harassment, anger management issues, drunkenness, and abuse of power. I'd had a couple of quiet concerns, but I was new to this denomination, to a church family of this magnitude and size. Jordan and I were dismayed at the rector's lack of repentance, his disregard for those he'd hurt and disappointed. He was ultimately removed from the congregation, defrocked from that church denomination. A scathing report from an outside organization further detailed his wrongdoing and cemented our own anger and confusion. (Just two years later, he would start his own church, right down the road from the cathedral, because of course.)

My point is, my cynicism didn't save me. It didn't prevent us from picking a church with a problematic pastor. It didn't protect my heart from more hurt.

We once again picked up the pieces of our fatigued faith, and maybe you're wondering why. There were times I did, too. Going to church felt so ridiculously stupid, like returning to the scene of the crime or going back to a bad boyfriend. And maybe I just kept going because that's what I'd always done. Old habits die hard, and so do old teachings and truths. I'd been raised to attend church every time the doors were open; a Sunday without church services felt foreign and disruptive to me, so maybe that's why I kept going.

I hope, though, I was also drawn to the sacraments, to quietly walking to an altar every week and reencountering the Jesus I so desperately needed and knew and loved. If everything and everyone else disappointed me, he remained, and I wanted a reminder to find him. Church, in all its inadequacies, did do that for me.

It reminds me, a little, of this phenomenon that occurs in my part of the world every spring and fall. On the very prettiest days of the very shortest seasons, my beautiful southern town and its clear blue skies will fill with gray billowing smoke from the pre-scribed burns of local acreage. I'll close my windows and will go on quicker, shorter walks, all to avoid the stench of smoke and burning.

This burning and its repercussions might be bad for me, but they are necessary for a flourishing land. "Good fires prevent bad ones," the Georgia Forestry Commission website warns, and I know, deep down, it's true, true in my life as well as in the life of the land. Sometimes things have to burn, but they don't stay charred and burned forever. After every burn season, I watch as things come back more vibrant than they were before. I drive by vast acreage with bright green grass poking up through the black and brown; flowers and leaves return anew, colorful and striking. My faith feels like a prescribed burn, and every few years, things I've thought were true are scorched to the ground. But by God's grace, my faith keeps blooming, keeps growing, keeps coming back, even when it makes no sense at all.

In the midst of my church upheaval and hurt, I was meeting with a spiritual director I'd found online. We'd talk on the phone once a month, when she'd lead me through Trinitarian breathing prayer and come alongside my questions. I brought up church a lot in those days, partly because we were still reeling from years of pain and disorientation, but also because I thought church was where God was, and I wasn't really feeling him there. I've never been one to trust my feelings, but not to feel God's presence at church felt like a red flag.

My spiritual director was not concerned.

Like Jordan with his happiness rating, she shrugged about the whole thing.

God's a lot of places, she reminded me. Church is only part of it.

I cannot stress enough how counterintuitive this realization was for me. It took me a decade to understand the immense pressure and expectation the denomination of my childhood put on church attendance and the institution of church itself. I'd been critical and cynical about church because church was important, maybe the most important.

Until it wasn't.

The stomachaches and headaches that used to accompany my Sunday-morning worship no longer exist, and it's not because I've found the right denomination or because the church we now attend is perfect. It's because I've put church in its proper place. I've lowered my expectations. I meet God everywhere, have grown to pay attention to him in every nook and cranny of my life. If a sermon is less than stellar or a prayer isn't prayed exactly how I'd pray it, I might be disappointed. I might have a question or two. I am still me, after all.

But I am no longer devastated when the church behaves in contradiction to itself.

The church is not Jesus.

Jesus is Jesus, and my expectations of him are met, every time.

My spiritual life no longer has church at its center. Do I still believe in church, still attend a church? Yes. Not everyone I love does, but I still do. I think one of the reasons this is even conceivable is because I lowered the bar.

I still want church to meet my expectations. In so much of my life, I want our institutions to do better, to behave better, to provide better. But much like I no longer worship a particular political party, I also no longer worship church. I do not have her on a high pedestal, because I see her for what she is: a motley group of people (sometimes) trying their best to believe in the unbelievable.

Some Sundays, I listen to a sermon I don't agree with. Some Sundays, my mind wanders. Some Sundays, I am offended by an ignorance toward global or national injustice. Some Sundays, I am disappointed by the convictions or political beliefs of a fellow churchgoer. Some Sundays, I am dismayed by a hymn I don't know or an awkward encounter with a fellow parishioner. Some Sundays, I am sad for what I have lost, for where the church has so obviously failed.

But every Sunday, I stand beside Jordan and among fellow believers and recite the words of the Nicene Creed. Every Sunday, I go forward and kneel at an altar and take bread and wine into my hands. Every Sunday, I pray for the people who have gone before me, for the people with power and the people without it. Every Sunday, I confess where I have failed in thought and word and deed. Every Sunday, I kneel for a moment in silence and think about how grateful I am to move my body in this way, to adopt a posture of worship in a world where it feels rare to do so.

A few years ago, I stopped expecting so much out of church. I started to be okay with a six on the happiness scale. I lowered the bar on my spouse, my friends, my family, my institutions, and myself. In a paradoxical turn of events, I think I am happier here, now. Of course I want more out of church, more out of my faith. But I now know perfection won't exist this side of heaven, whatever heaven may be.

So I find God in the cracker and the cup, in Jordan's hand holding mine, in my grandmother's favorite hymn. I find God in the cool spring breeze, in the expansive blue sky, in the way my puppy Sam traipses through a puddle. I find God while sitting in silence during spiritual direction, curling up in a family quilt, resting my head on my pillow at the end of a long day. I find God in a child's giggle and in a rose on a bush and in the eyes of my parents. I find God everywhere, so Sundays are simpler, less pressure. Lowering the bar changed my faith, shaped my life, opened my eyes to a wider expression and view of God.

What a relief.

# CHAPTER 13

# Be Ringo

I was a freshman in high school the year the Beatles' *1* album was released into the world. Whether I bought a copy or was gifted it, I can't be sure. My mom is a lifelong Beatles fan, but I generally bought most of my music myself. As evidence, the first CD I ever purchased with my own money was LeAnn Rimes's *You Light Up My Life*, a collection of inspirational covers, please someone tell me why.

The point is, I wasn't cool.

But listening to the Beatles at fourteen or fifteen made me feel cool. My peers were into punk rock—does "All the Small Things" count as punk?—but by my senior year I had the lyrics to *The Mary Tyler Moore Show* theme song printed in Sharpie on my messenger bag and "Let It Be" blaring from the speakers of my 1994 Nissan Sentra.

Singing about Mother Mary—a reference I wrongly concluded

was about Jesus's mother—on the way to my evangelical high school felt rebellious in a way I cannot fully describe to you now.

I played "Let It Be" until the song skipped, to this day the purest sign of musical devotion I know. I put the CD in my zip-up case (the same one still sitting in the back of my Subaru) and brought it out every so often throughout my college and early adult years. Nothing, though, matched the Beatles obsession of my teenage-hood, until the fall of 2021, when a pandemic still raged and Peter Jackson's *Get Back* released to streaming.

The multi-episode Beatles documentary didn't initially interest me. Few of my trusted pop-culture aficionados were discussing it, so I ignored it, too. It was eight hours in its entirety, too long to devote to any one work of art. But then I began hearing rumblings on a podcast I loved, and Jordan and I were in that weird stage between Thanksgiving and Christmas, when it's not really time for *It's a Wonderful Life* but also nothing new is being created and put into the world. We figured we'd try it, and if we didn't like it, we'd quit.

After the first installment ended, clocking in at around three hours long, I was ready for the second, and the third. I couldn't get enough, but I also didn't want to swallow it up entirely. I started it and didn't want it, the documentary or the band itself, to end.

Once we finished *Get Back* in full, I found myself fully immersed in an Enneagram 5 spiral, desperate for any thoughtful Beatles commentary I could consume. I downloaded audiobooks, watched interviews on YouTube, purchased special-edition magazines from the grocery store as if it were 2004 all over again. I could not get enough. I hadn't been this pop-culture obsessed since Greta Gerwig's 2019 adaptation of *Little Women*.

Why?

Was it nostalgia for my own teenage years, three decades removed from the Beatles' collapse? Was it a deeply held fascination with art and creativity and genius? An affinity for facial hair and bell-bottoms? An appreciation for sibling relationships and brotherly love?

All of the above, I'd guess. To sit in my living room and witness Paul McCartney—with major Kristy Thomas energy—sigh about John Lennon running late again, then grab his bass and riff until he found the rhythm for "Get Back" was absolutely stunning. I sat at my television in awe, then told literally anyone who would listen to me about it, never mind the fact that it's a famous piece of musical history, not something that occurred spontaneously yesterday.

It was a privilege to watch *Get Back*. It was like that fantasy we all have of being invisible and finding ourselves in the room where things actually really did happen. What a treasure for pop culture, and for music nerds everywhere.

Which brings me to Ringo.

If Paul is the cute one and John is the smart one and George is the mystical one, I suppose Ringo is the funny one? (Most commentators I've read simply describe him as the drummer.) Despite the undeniable genius of literally everyone in the room, I somehow couldn't keep my eyes off Ringo for much of the documentary, at first because I remembered he was my mother's favorite, and therefore he was most interesting to me, but then he became *my* favorite, though I'm sure if I took a Which Beatle Are You? quiz, I'd get Paul, not because of any artistic genius or talent but because of his clear type A personality. (Lots of "The group project is due tomorrow, guys!" energy.)

Ringo, though, mostly just minds his own business. He sits at his drums at the ready; in the documentary, he's never late for rehearsals, and he never complains. The only time he really offers his strong opinion throughout the entire recordings is to calmly state he wants to play live on the rooftop of 3 Savile Row, a quiet proclamation I'm convinced led to George himself being convinced. Without Ringo, would we even have that last live performance?

Back in December 2019, I saw Gerwig's *Little Women* and promptly adjusted my wardrobe accordingly. Now practically everything I own is Jo March–inspired, in one way or another.

In 2022, after witnessing Ringo's nonchalance in the *Get Back* recordings, I vowed to adopt his energy. If Jo March defined my wardrobe, I wanted Ringo Starr to define my vibe. I wanted to show up on time, mind my own business, and take things as they come. (I wanted to do this without the assistance of drugs.) I really wanted to be as laid back as that mustachioed percussionist, a reliable friend and an estimable musician who's content to be really good at what he does without necessarily having to be the center of attention. Paul and John are songwriting geniuses; without them, the Beatles and their music wouldn't exist. But without Ringo, I wonder if they'd have stayed together. You need, I think, the calm and funny one to survive the tumult of fame, and back in 2022, I knew I'd need to remain calm and funny to survive year three of a global pandemic.

Throughout that entire year, I found myself faced with one problem or conundrum after another, and every time, I'd whisper or mutter to myself, "Be Ringo." It became my mantra, my touchstone, my reminder to take a deep breath, to stay calm, to go with the flow. It's the very opposite of my bookstore energy. I want to be the definition of "chill" in the shop, but it comes more naturally to be the Paul McCartney energy in the room: to command, to make decisions, to take charge. Imagining Ringo sitting patiently at his drums helped me want to metaphorically sit at my drums, a lesson I've clung to in the years since.

While I was focused on channeling my inner Ringo, I was also meeting regularly with my spiritual director. I'd begun to meet with her in the fall of 2019, when I'd been outside the church of my childhood for six years. It felt, in some ways, like it had been forever, like Jordan and I had been attending liturgical church our whole lives. But we very much hadn't, and I was still struggling with my spiritual life, still floundering a bit, even though we'd finally settled on a new church home. I wondered if faith would come easily to me ever again. (Short answer: no, probably not.)

My spiritual director was helping me, back then, navigate my adult relationship with faith and with church and with God. She's still helping me, still whispering prayers over my life, speaking wisdom, asking questions, opening my eyes to truths I've buried, ignored, or forgotten. She's a good and gentle listener who sits with me in silence and points me, time and time again, back to God and back to myself.

Perhaps eight or so months into my Ringo obsession, my director and I were talking about Jesus, and she mentioned she'd once attended a conference with the theologian Dallas Willard. A student asked Willard for one single word he'd use to describe Jesus. Apparently, without hesitation, Willard replied: "Relaxed."

I flinched when she told me. *Relaxed*. Not loving, not generous, not truthful, not kind. Relaxed?

Ringo.

Of course, Jesus and Ringo are not one and the same. (Although, upon reflection, a '70s-era Ringo does look remarkably similar to a flannel-board Jesus.) But I do think there's something to Willard's answer, this idea that Jesus wasn't intense or brooding or constantly frustrated with his incompetent disciples. For some reason, I'd previously pictured him as a man who flipped tables in rage, a man who prayed so hard blood poured out of his flesh. But then I remember Jesus spent an inordinate amount of time sleeping on boats. He hung out with his friends and ate fish for breakfast. He told his mom to take a deep breath and to wait until the timing was right.

As my spiritual director quietly sat on the other end of the line, I wondered: *Was Jesus not an ambitious go-getter?*

The question makes me uncomfortable because I want to be like Jesus, but I'm only relaxed when I'm at home or on vacation. I try to be relaxed, and work and people get in the way. I don't know how to be relaxed when exterior pressures press in. I don't know how to maintain a state of relaxation in the face of my team or trauma or grief or gossip. When the world gets loud, I want to remain quiet, but I'm afraid I just get loud, too. I'm afraid I know how to relax only when it's calm and breezy, not when there's a storm afoot.

I long to be calm in the storm. I want to be Ringo when the band is about to break up.

This goes against my nature, especially in the imperfect world where we reside. This act of Ringo-ing, Jesus-ing, does not come easily to me, and I struggle. Being Ringo results in tears and exhaustion because it's rubbing up against every one of my natural inclinations.

Those inclinations were served well in the church of my childhood. The denomination where I first met Jesus was filled with loving, friendly people, but it was also deeply concerned with the rule-following aspects of faith. Scripture was something you could memorize and know deeply, something to be interpreted literally, a place where you could take your questions and, if you studied hard enough, receive actual answers back. There was little room for mystery, so my obedient, quiet nature fit for a while, until the questions I asked were no longer seen as precocious or curious but annoying and impertinent.

The rigidity of that church fit me for a long time. Until, in adolescence, it didn't.

When Jordan and I left the denomination well into our adulthood in 2013, it was painful and confusing and lonely, and I felt like I didn't know Jesus at all anymore. I found him, sometimes, in the whispers of liturgy or in the incense that wafted to the ceiling of our new cathedral, but I still mostly felt alone.

But then in spiritual direction, my director started referring to Jesus as my brother in our meetings. And I'd smile a little, because I love my brother. I know what a sibling relationship looks like, what it's like to have a brother who's goofy and funny and way more relaxed than I am. And I started to rethink the Jesus I thought I knew.

Because yes, Jesus did turn over tables, but really just the once. And that's kind of why it was a big deal? If Jesus spent most of his ministry in rage, the table incident would have been a blip. But it was shocking and startling and worth noting because it wasn't really in his standard repertoire of behavior.

Instead, Jesus was relentlessly calm. And it wasn't because he was some master at mindfulness (although maybe he was). I think it was because true relaxation occurs when we know ourselves and our purpose, when we're so confident in who we are that we can go through life without being plagued by worry, angst, or doubt. We are assured in our mission and our calling.

Ringo knew he was the drummer. He kept the beat, showed up on time, offered bits of feedback, paid attention to the artistry around him and responded accordingly. He was content to let Paul run the show. He knew who was in charge.

Jesus knew he was the son. His calling was clear, his mission tragic but life-changing and hope-filled for the rest of us. He did what he was told. He knew who was in charge, and he could rest in his identity.

Getting to know this assured, calm Jesus utterly changed my faith. He is my wise and funny brother, walking alongside me and urging me toward confidence, too. He longs for me to join him in his relaxed, easygoing posture. Deep breaths, quiet waters, light burdens. So different from the Jesus I thought I knew, but now that I know him this way, I long to be close. This is the faith I was craving while the rules and the theological warfare raged around me and inside me. The whole time, I was longing for a Jesus who took naps and smiled at me in peace.

"Be Ringo" is still something I whisper to myself, but now I think it's my soul's quiet way of pointing me toward Jesus, too. Relaxed? Oh, how I hope so.

# CHAPTER 14

# When Staying True Means Leaving, Redux

I went to the funeral of an old family friend last year. He and his wife had been two of my first bosses; as a teenager, I'd worked at weddings, assisting caterers and coordinators, and those events are still some of my fondest high school memories. I loved quietly observing the behind-the-scenes logistics that made those once-in-a-lifetime celebrations look like magic. I loved washing dishes while wedding guests danced in the background, loved maneuvering, unseen, in and out of people's best days. I wonder, today, if the reason I enjoy the quiet, behind-the-scenes responsibilities of the bookstore is because of those initial work experiences, watching Fran and Bobby ensure each wedding transpired gracefully and efficiently. Fran and Bobby and the way they managed events probably changed my life.

So I went to Bobby's funeral, even though millennials, traditionally, don't seem fond of funerals. I wonder, a little, if funerals themselves are a dying art, if the Covid years that deprived us of public grief and closure have changed how we say goodbye to the people we love. I don't like funerals, but I do think going to them matters. When my own grandmother died, I remember standing beside my parents, quietly accepting condolences as I saw two of my dearest friends walk through the doors of the church building. So few of my own peers attended that funeral that the attendance of those two sticks out. It occurred to me then how important it is to show up when you can. I've never forgotten the presence of those friends, their willingness to witness my grief, and now any time I can, I attend funerals, too.

I was hesitant, though, not simply because funerals can be awkward and tearful but because the funeral was being held at the church of my childhood and early adulthood, a place that had been excruciating to leave and had caused me immense hurt. It had also, for a long time, been home. It had been nearly a decade since I'd set foot in the building; the last time I'd been was for a different funeral, the funeral of a peer, so I was nervous. I was worried I'd walk in and be overwhelmed by hurtful memories, incapacitated by nostalgia and grief unrelated to my old boss or his death.

For hours, I debated going, all the while knowing I'd probably attend, because attending funerals is what stayers do. I'd go, and I'd sit with my parents, and I'd tease about the absence of my brother and cousins, people who never have to attend things like this because they left it all behind years ago.

I pulled into the parking lot, next to my aunt and uncle's car, and as predicted, I was filled with nostalgia. For years, I'd parked my Nissan Sentra in this very spot. I'd driven myself to church for Bible Bowl practices and singing nights and potlucks, and then I stopped. A stomachache not unlike the ones that had plagued me on Sunday mornings in early adulthood began to brew. The body, indeed, keeps the score, and as calm as I was on the outside, my inside was roiling. The aftereffects of church trauma are real, even when your trauma feels small compared to what others might have faced, even when "trauma" feels like too big a word.

Jordan had to work, so I walked into the church building alone, past the hill where I'd once sneakily sucked sweet nectar out of honeysuckle flowers, past the portico where I'd waited for a limo to pick us up for our church senior banquet, into the foyer where I'd asked my minister to pray for me because I had to fire someone. So many memories flooding my brain, I was simultaneously in overdrive and on autopilot.

Then, just like that, I was fine. I saw my parents in the crowd, greeted a couple who'd never failed to be nice to me or to them, not once in the years during or since our departure. The bitterness I'd expected to bubble back up never arrived. The stomachache from the parking lot dissipated. I didn't feel sad or overwhelmed. The nostalgia was there—I really did once call this place home, and that will never cease being true—but it didn't engulf me.

Instead, I saw warm, friendly, aging faces from my childhood, gave and received hug after hug after hug. Afterward, I realized it had been a long time since I'd been hugged like that by someone who wasn't my parent. Anglicans don't really hug, but also, no one hugs you like someone who probably once changed your diaper. No matter how long I attend our liturgical church, no one there will ever know me as Annie Sue Butterworth. They will never know me as Chris and Susie's daughter, as Carl and Annie Ruth's granddaughter. When I left my childhood denomination, I sacrificed those identities. The people I attend church with now are kind and loving, but they know me only as Annie, the woman who owns the bookstore. They might know me as Jordan's wife. But they don't know I once got in trouble for giggling relentlessly during a sermon. They don't know I refused to sit with the youth group for years because I didn't belong or feel comfortable. They don't know my entire family once took up two pews, or that I walked forward one Sunday morning and was baptized so I'd get to see my grandfather again.

It's unfair to ask anyone now to know me like that, so, for a couple of hours on a Friday afternoon, it was nice to be hugged by people who knew my grandparents. It was nice to be called *sugar* and *darlin'* by people who know I own a bookstore but who also don't really care. It was nice to be called Annie Sue, and to remember, at least for a little bit, who I used to be, how loved and cared for I once was.

It was also incredibly easy to leave. I sat in the pew with my parents just like I thought I would, but the hymns sung in four-part harmony didn't sound as beautiful as I'd remembered. The prayers were simple and sweet and quick, and I found myself missing the language of liturgy, found myself longing for the now-familiar words of the Book of Common Prayer. I got antsy during the short service, because my body is accustomed to standing and kneeling and bowing. My hands ached to complete the sign of the cross, an act that would have surely sent the polite Church of Christers around me to their early graves.

As the funeral ended and my parents and I walked to the parking lot together, we smiled at one another, because I think we'd all been waiting for feelings that never came. It wasn't hard to hug these people. It wasn't hard to love them. I think we forgave them a long time ago. We've lived a lot of life since we left, and as comforting as it is to be hugged by people who knew you way back when, it's also worth acknowledging they don't know you now.

When Jordan and I began attending the big cathedral, the one where we found respite after leaving this church behind, I commented to him how in the church of my origin in particular, I'd been loved but misunderstood. In the liturgical church, I felt understood—I finally felt like I was attending a church whose theology mostly (though, to be clear, not entirely) matched my personal convictions and beliefs—but not loved. This is not to say I felt unloved; no, I just felt anonymous. One of many. No one special.

In all my years at that ugly brown church on the hill, I'd never felt understood. I was an enigma, an oddball, a mystery. But for a long time and by many people, I was treated like someone who mattered, who was special, who was loved.

A lot of people, over the years, have left that church and then found themselves back between its walls, tethered by some invisible string. I feel no such tie. I think the reason I could smile and hug necks in genuine care and appreciation is because I am free. I am not bound by unforgiveness or anger or sadness. I am grateful for my time there. I learned some beautiful truths. I also learned a lot of things, so many things, I have spent years unlearning and untangling from the real things I know about Jesus.

You can't go home again, and I don't want to. But I think it is possible, with time, to return to the places you've left with grace in your heart, with appreciation for the good it gave you. I have a tendency to look on the past with rose-colored glasses. I can spend a lot of time wishing and hoping for things and places and people that no longer exist. (Did they ever?) But this former home of mine, the church of my origin, of my childhood and early adulthood—I think I finally see it clearly. My view isn't rosy or tinged by nostalgia or colored gray with anger. I am grateful for where I came from, for its stark simplicity, for its salt-of-the-earth people, for its warmth and care. But I am grateful and relieved for where I've wound up. I am free, without stomachaches and headaches. My relationship with church has changed, and leaving made it so.

I am glad I left, and I have healed enough to say I am glad that, for a little while, I stayed.

PART IV

# Staying Grounded

*You visit your hometown. You are driving aimlessly when you see the wall. You stop and slowly back up to the right-hand turn. It is built. There it is, all real and caked together with stones, and you feel a pang. You can get rid of everything else, the phone numbers and the photos, and still you will have these stories banging around inside you.*

—CJ Hauser, *The Crane Wife*

# CHAPTER 15

# The Front Porch

When I took over the bookstore back in 2013, one of the first ideas the store's then owner suggested to me was a podcast. She thought hosting a podcast would be a fun, unique way to introduce me to the town, a way to begin establishing credibility in my newfound community. Jordan and I both listened to podcasts on road trips, but I admittedly had no experience producing one. What I did have was a liberal arts degree, GarageBand on my computer, and enough gumption to go looking for a how-to video on YouTube.

A few months later, From the Front Porch was born.

I named the podcast because in my experience, the best, most thoughtful conversations in life occur on the front porch. To this day, the creaking of a porch swing is the sound that most reminds me of home, the sound that most brings me back to myself.

My parents bought the house they still own when I was ten and my brother was seven. Up until that point, we'd lived in a neighborhood down the street from my grandparents, my aunts, my cousins. It was, I thought then and still somewhat believe, the very best way to grow up. When my parents told us we'd be moving, I was devastated. We'd be only a five-mile car ride away from our old neighborhood, but it might as well have been the moon.

With time, though, my brother and I discovered we could play war in the sprawling backyard where my parents were having a few trees chopped down. There was a creek where we attempted to bury a dead armadillo, a basketball hoop in the driveway, and a family of horses right up the street. My room had two windows, and my parents put a desk in front of one so I could feel like my inspiration, John-Boy Walton.

And, of course, there was a porch: a vast, long wooden porch with stairs and a swing, eventually a cozy wicker couch on one end, ferns hanging between posts.

My mom has put in thousands of hours on that porch swing, swaying and praying. I received my first phone call from a boy while on the front porch—he was calling for help on his spelling homework—and had my first kiss there, too. At Thanksgivings and holidays, the kids' table would sometimes be on the porch, away from the watchful eyes of the adults, the slight whiff of freedom in the air. Throughout middle and high school, my mom and I would sit on the porch swing and talk about mean girls and hard days. She'd tell me life was a ruler, and this little part I was living was just a blip; it'd be over in a minute. When my brother, Chet, and I hung out in his bedroom, we'd hear the swing creak back and forth while my mom talked on the phone with her sisters, or my parents visited with each other, or my mother watched the birds. My parents sat me and my brother on the porch swing the day they told us my dad lost his job and family finances would be tight that year. They hosted my high school graduation brunch on the front porch. They moved the foosball table outside, and my friends came over, and we played and ate and laughed. On a cold January night right before I turned twenty-two, a boy I loved very much stuck a ring box inside a pair of Converse tennis shoes hiding on the front porch. He sat next to me on the swing, and we dreamed about life together. He proposed, I said yes, and in the weeks that followed, my mom and I planned a wedding from the comfort of the porch swing.

As a little girl, I loved—and now as a grown-up, I still love—my parents' front porch. I get weepy thinking about the day they'll eventually move, because the porch and the home they made for me and my brother means so much to me.

I think other people associate front porches with southern hospitality and being neighborly. I guess that's partially right. My parents wave to their neighbors from the front porch, and my mom has witnessed many an unfolding drama from its swing.

But I most associate the front porch with comfort and peace, a settled feeling you get only when you're content right where you are. To me, the porch represents long, rambling conversations with more questions than answers. It's honesty, vulnerability without the hangover. It's friends who are as close as family, and time un-spooling before you, not wasted but not cautiously spent.

Life slows down on the front porch; it's one of the only remaining places where this sentiment is real and true. When I drive the winding backroads to my parents' house—to the place I still think of, deep down, as mine—I can feel my burdens lifting, my breaths coming easier. Life is stressful, even in a small town, but as I make my way to my parents' front porch, I feel those stresses begin to dissipate. By the time I'm climbing up the steps to the swing, they've nearly disappeared entirely.

My parents have always been hospitable people. My father is a wonderful cook, and my mother can decorate and host a party deserving of a feature in *Southern Living*. But that's never fully encapsulated what I've meant by "hospitable." Hospitality isn't sparkling countertops and floral arrangements, though my mother is good at both of those things. Hospitality, to me, is a welcoming spirit, an arms-wide-open, everybody-belongs kind of mentality. Of course I feel strongly about my childhood home; I know very few people who don't. But over the years, the porch and its swing have meant something to other people, too, and that's because my parents have long greeted and soothed a variety of wandering souls from their spots on the swing. My cousin made big life decisions listening to my mother's wisdom on the steps of the porch; my childhood best friend remembers coming up those same steps and instantly feeling happy and at home. Once inside, she'd sit at the kitchen bar and visit with my parents, sometimes even before visiting with me. When my brother comes home from Tennessee, he gets up early with my dad, and they drink coffee on the porch together and watch the sunrise.

My parents' front porch is a happy place for a lot of people, and it's not just the creaking swing that makes it so. It's the two people who have greeted all sorts of life's fellow sojourners, always with open arms.

From the Front Porch, the podcast I helped launch and create more than a decade ago, now boasts more than five hundred episodes, with millions of downloads to its credit. It's absurd, how such a tiny thing never met its original purpose (Thomasville did not buy into podcasts until much later) but now serves as a significant marketing tool for the business I own.

Mostly, though, I hope From the Front Porch mimics the spirit created by the porch of my childhood. It's not the perfect podcast. I am hardly the perfect host. I don't feel nearly as wise or professional as Ira Glass, nor as funny as The Popcast, nor as prolific as Bill Simmons and The Ringer team. Industry-wise, our show is barely a drop in the bucket, a tiny little piece of podcast real estate.

But when people tune in, I hope they don't walk away with just book recommendations or ideas for growing their own small businesses. I hope they reach the end of an episode and feel a spirit of calm and contentment, like they've just finished talking to a good friend on a porch swing.

Years ago, a podcast listener asked what song best described the show. It didn't take me long to come up with an answer, perhaps because it's a bit on the nose. In "Front Porch," artist Joy Williams sings about the porch being a place you can come back to, no matter where you've been or what you've done or how long you've been gone. There's a spirit of welcome and respite on a front porch, and it's the kind of spirit I hope our show embodies, and I hope my home and my soul embody it, too.

My liberal arts degree prepared me for a life as a jack-of-all-trades, master of none. My journalism background equipped me with how to ask good questions and with a spirit of stick-to-itiveness. But it's my parents who raised me to be welcoming and open, honest and considerate, to embrace all types of people with hospitality and curiosity and warmth.

I don't have a porch swing in the home I live in now. It was a little disorienting, to start this chapter of our lives without one. But then I realized it's probably never really been about the swing. Maybe it's never even been about the porch. It's really about being a person who has time for other people, who listens well, and who sits and soothes and remembers life is a ruler, and this is all just a blip. It's about embodying the spirit of the porch and passing that spirit on to the people you love.

# CHAPTER 16

# Namesakes

There are a lot of things I like about myself. I like my natural hair color, my squinty smile when I'm at my happiest, my open-mouthed laugh, my love for the beach in the winter. But the thing I love most about myself might be my name.

Before I married Jordan, my name was Annie Sue Butterworth, and it's still, at least in part, how I think of myself. Jordan and I are a team, have been a team for a long time, so Jones does feel like a natural part of my identity. It's no longer as uncomfortable as I once found it. But before I was Annie B. Jones, I was Annie Sue Butterworth, painstakingly named for both my grandmothers, Annie Ruth and Linda Sue.

I can hardly type my name and theirs without tearing up, so proud and grateful am I for this name. I am convinced my stubbornness, my persistence, my creativity, my resourcefulness, stem from this name and the women who gave it to me. I don't fully know what possessed my parents to name their first daughter after their two mothers, but not a day goes by in which I am not grateful.

My grandmothers, it should be noted, were very different people, women of two disparate personalities. There were similarities, of course; both were women of a certain age and era, both grew up in small southern towns, got married young, stayed married, and had children. Both women took brave leaps of leaving, moving from their homes in Tennessee and Kentucky down to the godforsaken land of Florida, where they stayed and worked and raised families.

Here were the women as I knew them.

My mother's mother, Annie Ruth, was short, petite, and, eventually, round. Growing up, she would tease me about my own smallness, lamenting our collective inability to reach items from tall shelves, but quick to remind me dynamite comes in small packages. She sewed matching outfits for me and my American Girl dolls, including an Easter dress with the puffiest puff sleeves you can possibly imagine. (Anne Shirley and any number of shepherdesses would have been impressed.) She had quite the extensive doll collection herself, and whenever I see a forlorn doll in an antique store, I, of course, am struck by its creepiness, but I am also sad, because my grandmother thought dolls were precious, and she treated hers—the ones she bought and the ones she made—with such care. I am not sure I have ever cared for any one object with such tenderness and pride.

My grandmother was creative; her creativity was passed down

to my mother, to my aunt, to me, to my cousin. I see her finger-prints in our homes, in our clothes, in the way we place a pillow or are stopped in our tracks by something eye-catching and beautiful. My grandmother appreciated beauty.

She was the only sister of two brothers. I grew up in admiration and awe of my mother's relationships with her sisters, but I was also a little jealous of this bond I didn't fully understand and never would have. In my grandmother's ninetieth year, my mom and I escorted Mama to the funeral of her dear friend. We sat next to her in the somber quiet of the church, and I couldn't help but think of how painful it must be to watch as your friends all leave you behind.

As we filed out of the funeral together, I listened to my grandmother stop and say to anyone who would listen: "She was my little sister." My dad, standing nearby, commented, "You're part of a sisterhood, aren't you?" She looked at him and nodded emphatically, acknowledging yes, she had a sisterhood.

Because if you don't have sisters, you form a sisterhood of your own. I've formed mine in dear friends and kindred spirits and cousins. My grandmother taught me how.

She was giving and generous, devoting her time and energy to writing cards to the sick and grieving, to making teddy bears for the local hospital. She did not stop for a moment until her death. Her hands were always busy. She loved her soap operas and long phone calls, and my mother reminds me so much of her.

My father's mother was, in my mind, taller, more glamorous, and more introverted than Mama, my mother's mother. She loved throwing dinner parties and entertaining and setting a pretty table. Those parties I threw in my twenties? Mama B. helped me host those. The first time I cooked lamb, I called her, and she walked me through it. She played golf and bridge, and she and my grandfather joined country clubs where in the summers we would swim in pools and eat chicken tenders at the occasional buffet. Sometimes, we were even allowed to drive a golf cart or two; often, we were encouraged to bring a friend.

My grandmother adored sports on television, and even though I've always thought my love for March Madness came from my father, I'm realizing I grew up watching a woman be interested in sports—in basketball, in tennis, in golf, in football—and in rooting for her various teams. She often had one sporting event or another on a television in the background just for the noise of it, and now I do, too. She was loyal and opinionated and quick-witted and devoted to her friends, some of whose names I still somehow have tucked away in my memory: Royce Anne. Marnita. Margie. Patsy. With every girls' trip I take, I am building on the legacy Mama B. set for me.

After my grandfather's death, Mama B. lived alone. She went to church and to the movies, and she still played bridge. She's who taught me how to shuffle cards. I never once thought playing cards were the work of the devil, and I suppose I can thank my grandmother for somehow saving me from that piece of an evangelical upbringing.

If I am welcoming and friendly, it is Annie Ruth. My mother's mother. Mama. If I am witty and independent, it is Linda Sue. My father's mother. Mama B.

Neither of my grandmothers is here anymore. None of my grandparents are. If I think about it too much, I get bogged down by this sadness, this grief, that my own children won't get to meet these people who shaped so much of who I am. But then I remember my children will have me. I am the living embodiment of Annie Ruth and Carl, Linda and Charles, and it will have to be enough.

For much of my childhood, I grew up just a few doors down from my mother's parents. Mama and Papa were some of the earliest mentors and caregivers I had; in fact, my brother and I never had a babysitter, never were under the care of anyone not related to us. I never thought of this as anything but normal. So it should not be surprising that I grew up loving dolls and doll clothes, Braves baseball and piano music, the Gaither gospel hour and the cheapest cookies you can buy at the grocery store. These are the things my grandparents loved, so I loved them, too.

When Mama died in January 2012, I was living in Tallahassee, fully immersed in adulthood. I was married with a job, but I also lived in my hometown, not far from where my grandmother lived, too. I saw her at least once a week, every week, for church or family dinners. When she fell one wintry night, it wasn't a faraway phone call, a plane ticket purchased in frantic despair. It was tangible, the hospital just minutes from my house and my work. I could see the grief imprinted on my mother's and aunts' worried faces, could read the fear in my cousins' eyes. In the weeks following her fall, I used my lunch breaks to take sandwiches to the hospital, to give my mom and aunt a hug, to sit with my grandmother while visitors streamed in and out of her room.

It all happened in the blink of an eye and felt like it dragged on for years. I had no idea just how long death could take, how unyielding the human body can be, even when it's worked hard for over ninety years.

Both my grandmothers lived on this earth for a long time. It can feel selfish to grieve losses like that, when some people get far fewer days. Both my grandmothers were at my wedding. They got to meet Jordan, knew the adult version of me. A rare and wonderful gift, to be sure, but it doesn't make their absences any smaller.

I am comforted by the ways they both live on in me, by memories that come flooding back, depending on the day. I love nothing better than sitting around with my family, reminiscing about the people we loved, wondering where they might be and what they might think of us now. We laugh about the time Mama B.'s friend was driving her to a movie, worriedly commenting on how the film they were set to see might be inappropriate. My grandmother rolled her eyes and made her friend turn the car around; they were "too old" to be worrying about whether or not a movie was appropriate. My grandmother was annoyed, so she went back home. This story, my family laughs, could easily be one about me.

There are some days when I'll spot a white-haired woman out at a restaurant, moving slowly, her arm held by someone who is clearly her daughter. My throat will catch and my eyes will fill, because it reminds me so much of my mother and grandmother. I know those people. I have been those people.

There is another kind of moment, too, one that hasn't happened in a while, and I wonder if I've experienced it for the last time without noticing. Occasionally over the years, I would be working in the bookstore, and I'd overhear someone asking for "Annie Sue." My staffers weren't sure such a person existed. I've gone by Annie since college, not for any reason, just for ease, really. I never even thought about why I dropped my middle name. But the people who've known me longest never dropped it. To them, I'm still Annie Sue. When I hear that double name come out of someone's mouth, I poke out from whatever corner I've been hiding, from wherever I've been shelving books, and I wonder whom I'll see. Who knew me then? Do they know me still? Will they recognize the adult version of me? Will the name they know match the face I now have?

A legacy exists far beyond and outside a name. I know this. But for me, my grandparents' legacy is wrapped up in the name I've carried since childhood. It could have felt like pressure. It never did.

Instead, my name is one of the most comforting parts of myself. It's an honor and a privilege to take these women with me every day, to feel them sloshing around inside me somehow. I feel connected to them, decades after their deaths, and I think it's partly because their names are also mine.

Linda and Annie Ruth showed me there are many different ways to be a woman. Their distinct personalities and callings helped me know there are a thousand right ways to mother, a thousand right ways to be a person in this world. They loved me in their own distinct ways, too, Mama teaching me how to cross-stitch and patching up my treasured stuffed animals, Mama B. taking me to the movie theater and making sure my cousin and I got a week together every summer.

In the fifth grade, I—like thousands of Floridian children before me—competed in the Tropicana Speech Contest. When I was growing up, the contest was a rite of passage, something you had nightmares about and dreaded for years before ever attempting yourself. You had to write and prepare a three-minute speech about the topic of your choice. I loathed the thought of standing in front of my classmates, looking into their eyes, imagining them in their underwear. Speechmaking, I felt sure, was not for me. Speech writing, though? That I could do.

I set out to write the best three-minute speech Tropicana had ever seen, and the title I chose for my masterpiece was "My Two Papas," a phrasing I was proud of then and now.

My speech was devoted to my two grandfathers, their similarities and differences, and how both had been passed down to me. I thought my grandparents were interesting people, and I was fascinated by the ways we were connected, by the parts of me I felt could be traced directly back to them. Looking at them, I thought, could maybe point me to my future, could show me who I might one day become.

This essay, I suppose, is the adult version of my Tropicana speech. All these years removed from elementary school, and I'm still obsessed with tracing parts of me—my personality, my decision-making, my tastes, my work—back to the people who went first. It's reassuring to know maybe I'll turn out okay, because my grandparents did. Maybe my life will be long, like theirs, and I'll get to live out all the dreams I still have for my future. Maybe I have plenty of time.

These days, fewer and fewer people call me Annie Sue. Members of my grandmother's generation often would accidentally slip and call me Annie Ruth. I loved it, and it never happens anymore. The time for those slips of the tongue has long passed.

But inside, Annie Sue is my name. It's my identity. It's a part of me that's never changed, not in nearly forty years. I hope in forty more, I feel the same way—still rooted, still connected—to the people who loved and knew me first.

CHAPTER 17

# Everybody Writes About Sisters

Until I'd read Ann Patchett's *Commonwealth*, I'd always preferred her nonfiction to her fiction. I loved the way she formulated her thoughts and stories into profound, funny essays, but it wasn't until *Commonwealth* that I appreciated what her imagination could do. Then, in 2019, she released *The Dutch House*.

*The Dutch House* consumes my memory, not because it has a gorgeous cover (though it does), or because it's a wonderful work of dysfunctional family fiction (it is). I fell in love with it almost instantly, because it's a sibling story narrated by a younger brother, Danny, about his sharp older sister, Maeve. Do you know how few stories exist about a brother and a sister? As a child, I read books about orphans or only children or sisters or brothers or households teeming with children. I read about the March sisters and Ramona and Beezus and the Hardy boys and the Ingalls girls; as a teenager, I finally encountered Scout and Jem, but Scout was a pesky younger sister with a protective older brother, and I still felt like no one's story looked like mine.

In 1988, my parents brought home my little brother, Chet, and I promptly threw all his tiny newborn clothes in the big black trash can outside. I was uninterested in baby dolls and therefore also uninterested in babies (a personality quirk that would persist until . . . oh, still). I'd been doing just fine on my own, and a new baby felt disruptive to the order of things. In family videos, you can see my face scrunch together in pain when he cries, my attempts to sit and be gentle before I immediately become bored. I think I would have said, "Call me when he's a little older," if I could.

As the years progressed, my brother and I fell into a rhythm. I became bossy, self-assured. He'd go along with my plans and provide our family with much-needed comic relief. I hadn't wanted a younger sibling, but I think I'd needed one: someone to take the pressure off, to remove any extraneous attention. A partner in crime, a playmate. And although I would have preferred a sister—or, better yet, a twin (blame a '90s obsession with the Olsens and *The Parent Trap*)—my brother and I got along swimmingly, mostly. We played together, often taking turns between my interests and his: American Girl dolls and school for me, LEGOs and anything outdoors for him. And sometimes there existed a Venn diagram–esque overlap, like when we both played basketball throughout elementary and middle school.

But this isn't an essay about how my childhood was shaped by my brother.

It's an essay about how my adult self is better for having a brother, even if no one besides Ann Patchett really talks about brother-sister dynamics.

Years ago, on my life-changing trip to London, our little tour group sat around talking about our family dynamics. There were eight of us on that trip, three guides and five participants, all engaged in varying degrees of entrepreneurship and creativity. I had never met any of these women, and one of my fears before I left was that I wouldn't be able to connect with anyone; the trip was so short, and I am, typically, slow to engage. I am good at lifelong community building but less skilled at short-term relationships. (This is one of the many reasons I was not cut out for summer camp.) So I was nervous and worried, and I spent the weeks leading up to our departure praying God would let relationships come easily for me that week, that I would be able to be vulnerable and open and honest with these women I'd never met.

By the third or fourth day, I felt bonded. I didn't know if I'd stay in touch with these women forever, but I knew we were experiencing something special together, and as we sat around and talked about our families of origin, we attendees realized, startlingly, we all had something in common: we were all elder sisters to younger brothers.

My entire life, I've been friends with girls from large families or friends with only children or friends with girls who have sisters. I've rarely, if ever, been able to understand any of those dynamics because they are so different from my own. But as I sat around with this random group of women in London, I was filled with a deep understanding. No wonder I could connect so quickly with these people I'd never met. Deep down, there was an existing commonality. Deep down, we'd been raised the same, at least in part. Deep down, we were elder sisters with little brothers, which meant we were bossy, but also low-key. Brothers, I am convinced, help lower the temperature in the room, help with any high-strung, high-maintenance tendencies an eldest daughter might have. They bring the seriousness we possess down a notch.

Sisters are meant to be best friends. Every woman I know with a sister is best friends—or at least close friends—with her sister. They talk or text every day; even if they live far away, they sometimes dress in the same clothes by accident or order the same food at restaurants. My mother is best friends with her sister. I grew up bearing witness to it, hearing my mom swing back and forth on the porch swing talking to my aunt Lisa for hours on end. I assumed, at some point, Chet and I would be the same, forgetting that a brother-sister bond is quite different from a sisterly one.

My brother is not my best friend. His best friend is someone named Russ. (Hi, Russ!) They've known each other since kindergarten, and when Chet comes back home to visit, seeing Russ is always a top priority, maybe even more of a priority than seeing me.

This used to bother me, but as I've gotten older, I adore my brother's lifelong friendship with Russ. My brother isn't my best friend, but he is my best brother. We text at random intervals about things we remember from childhood or current church aches and pains or our jobs or our families or politics. I tried, for a while, to schedule monthly phone calls with Chet. Neither one of us is great on the phone, but I saw how my friends communicated with their sisters, and I thought I was failing at sibling love.

I wasn't.

My brother and I show our love for each other differently than my mother and her sisters do. There are very few hours-long heart-to-hearts, no weekend getaways without the kids and no fiery arguments or tearful make-ups. Instead, one time, my brother hid a minibar's worth of tiny liquors in my suitcase as I was packing for a weekend with my in-laws. I don't drink, which was half the joke, and I could not stop laughing. When I started grad school, I was worried about finding a parking space in the middle of the day on such a large university campus, so Chet would pick me up from my work and drop me off in front of my building.

The summer before my brother's senior year of high school, he wanted to go to a concert at a local bar, but my parents wouldn't let him go without a chaperone. I drove us down to the Beta Bar, a graffiti-covered building near downtown Tallahassee that no longer exists, much to my brother's dismay. As we entered the bar, my brother stopped at a bucket filled with earplugs. "You're gonna need these," he said, and I was incensed. I was cool! I was only nineteen! I didn't need earplugs at a concert. The band started playing, and I immediately put the earplugs in my ears. *This* is what the brother-sister bond looks like. I will go to your concert and stand in the back, and you will give me earplugs because you know I need them. We will do these things because we are really different people who really love each other.

Of course, we are also remarkably similar. Chet can quote *When Harry Met Sally* and *You've Got Mail* with impressive ease. We both love basketball, though I prefer college and Chet prefers the NBA. I understand *Star Wars* and *Dragon Ball Z* references, and for a while there, Chet knew all the Bath & Body Works scents by name. We're both #TeamJess, and if we ever need to confirm a childhood memory—"What was the name of that song?" "Who was that awful kid in Sunday school?" "Remember when Dad got mad about Taco Bell?"—we know we're just a text away. My grown-up house is always just a little bit messy, proof I was raised sharing a bathroom with a boy. Chet's grown-up house is pristine, proof he was raised sharing a bathroom with a girl.

The other night I went to a performing arts event with a friend. We were talking before the show, speculating as to how type A we both are. She's a local educator; I run the indie bookstore in town. There's an assumption, I think, that we would both be highly organized, competitive, ambitious perfectionists. There may be some truth to that, particularly if you don't know me super well. But my friend and I were both discussing how there's also a part of us that doesn't look type A at all; we roll with the punches and pivot quickly when we need to. We both decided our jobs—which require a lot of improvisation—must have made us this way.

Then I remembered she has a brother.

You cannot convince me that brothers don't make their sisters more relaxed versions of themselves. My brother was never impressed by my grades or my ambition or my talent. He didn't care, and not in an unkind or ugly way. Brothers don't care about that stuff, and I think we sisters are better for it. When we were little, my brother cared what sort of playmate I was, whether I would sit in his room at his LEGO table and create stories and build worlds together. As we got older, he cared that I could drive, that I could take us to school or to the movies or to church, that I could guarantee his own independence would arrive a little earlier than my own had.

When I graduated from high school and left home, I didn't realize, fully, that I'd be leaving him. This was simply the order of things. You turn eighteen, and you go to college. You move. You leave.

Now as someone who has been left over and over and over again, I understand more fully how hard this must have been on my younger sibling. But he never seemed mad or upset. Instead, he came to my Podunk university campus and spent the night in my boyfriend's dorm room and cheered for me while I played flag football. I think unknowingly, without even trying, he taught me how to stay, how to root for someone when it's their turn to go. How to recover and remain yourself when the people you love go somewhere else.

My brother now lives six hours from me. It is one of the cruelest facts of my adult life, which I know hints to you the privilege with which I am living. I always imagined my brother would live down the road, just like my mother's sisters had. But when Chet graduated college, it was his turn to go, and my turn to stay.

I often wish I could turn back time and drive my brother to school again. I wish we could laugh together and karaoke to

Relient K in my Nissan with the windows cranked down. I wish we could sit on my couch and binge *Gilmore Girls* or *Arrested Development*.

I wish we could do those things, because to this day, there is no one who can make me laugh like he can. There is no one who so immediately lowers my blood pressure, who helps me settle into myself. I think it's partly because I miss male friendship. I miss the ease of it. At college, many of my friends were guys, and it's not because I was a tomboy or hated women or was trying to make some weird feminist (or antifeminist?) stand. It was because I was used to having my brother around. I didn't date these men. I truly wanted to be their friend, a sister figure. That was the role I was good at. That was the role I knew I could play.

This is the role I miss most in adulthood. I miss being a big sister to a younger brother, miss being a little bossy and a little bit funny. I miss these parts of me because they exist most fully when my brother is around.

For much of my childhood, I longed for a sister. When I got married, I was thrilled Jordan had one. Here was my chance to finally have the thing I'd always wanted, the relationship I'd always craved. But Jordan's sister was used to having a brother, and I was, too. Brothers are easier, and I've grown up and realized I wasn't cut out for sisters. I'm not emotionally equipped, don't have enough feelings. I was meant for a brother, and a brother is what I got.

No one writes about big sisters and little brothers, so I wanted to. I wanted to tell our story because it's one of my very favorites to tell. If you have a brother, I bet you understand.

# CHAPTER 18

# A Marriage Story

My senior year of high school, when word spread I'd be attending a Christian college, a man at my church asked me if I'd be getting my MRS degree. Somehow, in my eighteen years, I'd never heard that joke before, and I wrongly assumed he was asking me about a master's degree program. Once he had to explain the joke—which I hope, to this day, he's a little embarrassed by—I was livid. I was eighteen! Nora Ephron raised me! Sure, I believed in the romantic comedy, but I had things to do first. Marriage was one of the furthest things from my independent, baby-feminist mind.

The first week on our Alabama campus was reserved for freshmen only. It was very "summer camp," which outside of *The Parent Trap*, is my personal nightmare. There were icebreaker activities, a ropes course, a trust fall . . . basically a Mad Libs of leadership training for young adults embarking on their next chapters. I hated every minute of it, except for the minutes we were in a classroom.

I was born for the classroom. I love learning, love taking notes, love sitting still, love a buzzing-with-intellectual-energy atmosphere. I'd picked this university not for my future marriage's sake, but for its Great Books program, a rigorous course of study that relied on the Western canon and conversations held around a giant table. It was exactly what my younger self had pictured college to be, which was nice, considering the campus itself was not exactly inspired by the Ivy League. Founded in 1942, my alma mater is named not after American author William Faulkner—as I'll often allow people to believe—but after the somewhat-lesser-known Church of Christ minister Jimmy Faulkner, please bless it. When I set foot in the campus library for the first time, I wanted to weep in despair. It was, in a word, bleak, smaller than a single branch of my hometown public library, and hardly a place I wanted to spend any time.

Faulkner became mine despite all the reasons it shouldn't have, because I loved that gigantic oblong table, and, in a twist I couldn't have predicted, I'd also wind up loving the guy sitting two seats down from me.

That's right. I went to college to become the next Barbara Walters and instead met my future husband the first week of school. I was furious the budding comedian at my childhood church would be proven right.

As much as I hated the first week on campus, Jordan was in love with it. Homeschooled in his teen years, Jordan had not one trace of awkwardness. He was funny and goofy and personable, and he didn't seem to hate anything. He was game for all of it, the icebreakers, the trust falls, never rolling his eyes or expressing regret or dismay. He was surrounded by friends almost instantly, and I, lonely immediately after my parents and brother drove away, was envious.

He seemed to move comfortably through the campus, and he was always, from the very first day I met him, completely himself.

I did not fall in love with Jordan the first week of school. I'm not sure I, as a person, am capable of love at first sight. I just wanted to be his friend. I had other friends, too, friends in the theater program (those who can't act paint sets and write newspaper reviews), friends in the so-tiny-as-to-almost-be-nonexistent journalism department, and friends and acquaintances galore from the aforementioned Great Books classes. But Jordan became my best friend, quickly. Most of my friendships across the story of my life have taken weeks, months, and years to cultivate. And I know college, of course, amplifies, intensifies, and expedites all sorts of relationships. But meeting Jordan was, I think, the first time I ever met a person and thought: *Oh! You! I've been waiting for you.*

In *The Four Loves*, C. S. Lewis explains that friendship doesn't simply happen of our own volition:

> *In friendship . . . we think we have chosen our peers. In reality, a few years' difference in the dates of our births, a few more miles between certain houses, the choice of one university instead of*

*another . . . the accident of a topic being raised or not raised at a first meeting—any of these chances might have kept us apart. But, for a Christian, there are, strictly speaking no chances. A secret master of ceremonies has been at work. Christ, who said to the disciples, "Ye have not chosen me, but I have chosen you," can truly say to every group of Christian friends, "Ye have not chosen one another but I have chosen you for one another." The friendship is not a reward for our discriminating and good taste in finding one another out. It is the instrument by which God reveals to each of us the beauties of others.*

This is what best articulates how I feel about meeting Jordan.

Our first semester, we read *Nicomachean Ethics* together—a confession so nerdy I can barely type it—and that first Christmas, I gifted him a book of assorted writings from the early church fathers, an act that should have easily foreshadowed for our parents our eventual deviation into the liturgical church.

Our love story is not particularly groundbreaking or exciting or even romantic. We didn't experience a rom-com meet-cute like the ones I grew up assuming I'd have. Perhaps the literary couple we most see ourselves in is lifelong competitive frenemies Anne Shirley and Gilbert Blythe, only I've never hated Jordan. We were friends for a long time, so long that to this day neither of us is ever quite sure when we had our first official date. We went from friends to dating rather effortlessly; not because we were particularly effortless people but because when two absent-minded professors get together, does either of them really know what day? It was something in my life that came naturally, surprisingly, since dating and romance were not things in which, at eighteen, I had much experience.

I did not intend to be one of those raised-in-purity-culture millennials who married the first person she seriously dated; after all, I'd thrown my copy of *I Kissed Dating Goodbye* across the room in disgust. But I also was a late bloomer with little interest in romance outside of pop culture, dating only occasionally in high school. When I met Jordan, I wasn't thinking whether he was marriage material. I only thought that, of all the people on our campus, he was the person who made the most sense to me. He sometimes had to repeat his sentences because his Alabama accent was so thick, but for the most part, I understood him. Being his friend was easy, and dating was mostly easy, too.

There were a few issues, of course; everyone has them. We're both competitive, though Jordan is—shock to no one—more easygoing, so when he attempted to teach me how to play tennis, I became so irritated I pulled a John McEnroe and threw the racket down in rage. (I do not like being talked down to or spoken to with any authority, really ever, and Jordan is a natural teacher. You do the math.) When our college courses overlapped, we'd study together, comparing grades on pop quizzes and exams. I don't think we were ever obnoxious about it, but I also recall arguing and debating over which professors liked which one of us best, so . . . maybe we were.

As we spent more and more time together, though, I noticed Jordan had a few spiritual hang-ups I didn't have. I'd always been a bit of a Goody Two-shoes, despite my best efforts. I obeyed rules, read my Bible, took my faith seriously. My upbringing had, I now know, made me more than a little legalistic. Then I met Jordan, who a few months into dating informed me we had to stop holding hands. "I'm worried what my future wife might think," he told me apologetically, and although I figured she probably wouldn't mind, I agreed to stop. We didn't have to hold hands, or frontally hug, or kiss. Whatever. I wasn't worried about Jordan's future wife; if he was, that was fine. We'd figure it out.

Years later—when Jordan's future wife became me, his present one—other minor obsessions like this presented themselves, and they often were similarly irrational. Jordan is smart and funny and kind, and his quirky rule-following didn't make sense to me; it had stopped feeling idiosyncratic and had become stifling, overwhelming. I was frustrated; Jordan was frustrated, so in our early days of marriage, we decided he needed to see a psychiatrist, who eventually diagnosed him with OCD. I was confused by this diagnosis. I'd known a girl in college who had OCD, and she had to make sure the light switches in a room were all flipped the same way. Jordan doesn't notice details, ever, so he's certainly not bothered by them. But shortly after his OCD diagnosis, Jordan and I were on a road trip, listening to *This American Life*. The episode was about confessions, and Ira Glass was interviewing a Catholic priest about something called scrupulosity. "Scrupulosity," Glass reflected, "is when somebody obsesses over whether he is doing things that are sinful. It causes anxiety. The person can't stop thinking about it. . . . Father [Thomas] Santa says that it can be paralyzing for people. It can make the smallest decisions impossible."

Jordan and I looked at each other in immediate recognition. It's one of the only times in my life I feel like I've truly experienced an epiphany.

Naming something takes away its sting. It's why I've always loved how Dumbledore isn't afraid to say Voldemort's name in the Harry Potter books. ("Always use the proper name for things. Fear of a name increases fear of the thing itself.") Naming Jordan's scrupulosity made it a known entity, something we could work on together, and it no longer felt lonely, at least to me. Listening to that podcast episode, I realized there were other people like Jordan in the world, and—this was important—I wasn't "less Christian" for not spotting potential sin around every corner.

I'd spent our college years wondering, off and on, if the problem was me, if I wasn't spiritual enough to date someone as "good" or as "holy" as Jordan.

And I'd like to be clear: Jordan *is* good. He is thoughtful and patient in ways I wonder if I will ever be. But he is not perfect, and his goodness has nothing to do with his former obsessions over sin and behavior. He is good because God is good, and God lives in Jordan.

I've digressed now, from our love story. But it was important for me to hear OCD and scrupulosity named, so I wanted to name them here, too. I wanted to identify what was, for us, a real hardship in our early days, something few people in our day-to-day life understood. I never wanted to embarrass Jordan, so I never wanted to talk about something he wasn't comfortable talking about. Over the years, discussing his scrupulosity has come more naturally to us, and we've encountered other couples dealing with similar issues, and it's always such a relief. Talking openly about things can, actually, make them easier.

Jordan and I are now rapidly approaching middle age. We've known each other for more than half of our lives, a statistic I could barely register when we were eighteen and trust falling into each other.

No marriage is easy; two people choosing to grow up and older together across time and shifts in ideology and identity sounds a little foolish, in fact. But I'd be lying if I said my marriage to Jordan was hard. Jordan is still the person in my life who makes the most sense. We're no longer on a tiny Christian college campus, far from it, but I still look out in a crowd, spot Jordan, and think: *Oh, yes. There he is. Here is the person who will talk me down off life's ledge, who will help ground me when I'm feeling unmoored.*

A friend of ours once described relationships as "start-ups" or "mergers." Start-ups, he said, are for folks who get married young, combining every aspect of their lives—finances, yes, but other things, too—because they've barely become individual people. Mergers describe most modern marriages: two fully formed adults combining assets, both literal and figurative.

Jordan and I were, of course, a start-up. We barely had anything to our individual names; I was still a credit ghost when we bought our first house. We've grown up together, and I know not every marriage survives that process. When I look back at our twenty-two-year-old selves on our wedding day, I think: *Who let us do that? What was everyone thinking?* If we have children one day, I'm not sure how I would feel if they chose marriage at twenty-two. I wonder if I'd be afraid they might miss out on something great, if the hardships would be too challenging to overcome, if they'd even know themselves at all.

I'd like to think Jordan and I did know ourselves. We've always been a little elderly on the inside, so maybe we were more mature than our twenty-two years suggested. But even if we knew ourselves, we couldn't have known what the years would hold: leaving the church of our childhoods, disappointing friends and loved ones. Attending law school, then grad school. Moving to a small town. Living far away from our siblings. Buying a bookstore. Traveling around the world. Losing loved ones. Realizing children might not be in the cards.

Life is hard. I guess I could look back and wonder what twenty-two-year-old Annie was thinking. I could imagine that if I hadn't gotten married, I could have moved to the big city of my dreams and become a journalist for the *New York Times*. But instead, I often find myself looking back and wanting to say thank you to that twenty-two-year-old version of me: Thank you for getting married. Thank you for choosing Jordan. Life *is* hard, and I'm so glad and grateful to do it with Jordan by my side.

Our marriage is not perfect, but it is ours. I was wondering, while writing this, if there is anything magical or mystical about our marriage, or if it is practical, pull-yourself-up-by-your-bootstraps work. I imagine it's both. I do think it's a little magical and mystical, how two eighteen-year-olds could have seen in each other a future worth having. And every day, there's work involved, too. Laundry and dishes and making the bed. Deciding which TV show will lull us to sleep on any given evening.

I may not have gotten the meet-cute, or the New York City walk-and-talk. But as it turns out, I have experienced the future Kathleen Kelly and Joe Fox once dreamed about. I have lived a deliciously ordinary life and marriage: drinks, dinner, a movie . . . for as long as we both shall live.

# CHAPTER 19

# Life Without Children

For over a year, Jordan has been tracking my ovulation on a phone app with dedication and precision I do not feel. It's exhausting work, monitoring one's fertility, and despite my age, I have not always approached it with the degree of seriousness I reserve for my life's other callings. Honestly, after teenage years filled with fear about everything from tampon insertion to unwanted pregnancy, it's a miracle I've wanted to attempt sex and motherhood at all.

Throughout my thirties, I've been meeting with a therapist and a spiritual director, and although my work there has most often been devoted to my actual work, in my more vulnerable sessions and in my more desperate moments, I've confessed to my confusion regarding children and motherhood. As a young girl, I expected I'd become a wife and mom, but I never was very concerned about it. Those roles and identities did not weigh heavily, or even anywhere, on my list of things I wanted to be and do. When I met Jordan, I know we talked about kids, and I know we figured we'd have them. But I didn't intend to get married at twenty-two, and once married, having children was not a priority. We were so young. Jordan was in law school; I was our family's breadwinner, and adjusting to married life was hard enough. There was plenty of time to think about children.

But over the years, I didn't really think about it. I didn't feel particularly passionate about the timing of children or motherhood. When Jordan's younger sister got married years after we did, she confessed to wanting to get pregnant sooner rather than later. "Don't you want your parents to be alive to be grandparents?" she asked me. "Don't you want to be a young mom?"

The grandparent question was admittedly troubling to me, but I was not concerned with being a youthful mom. That ship had sailed, and my own mother hadn't had me until she was thirty, so my internal clock didn't really begin ticking until then. Even after that life milestone, I remained hesitant. It'd be easy to blame my ambivalence on the bookstore. Running and operating the shop consumed most of my time and energy throughout my twenties and thirties, and it's common to blame a woman's career for decisions regarding family planning. But when we took over the bookstore, we specifically—though perhaps naively—discussed how great this new career could be if I became a mom. How, really, entrepreneurship might give me the flexibility I needed to later pursue motherhood. If anything, the shop helped me realize I might be able to juggle becoming a mother; if you can run a business, I think you might be capable of doing anything.

So the bookstore and my career, despite people's assumptions, really had very little to do with my hesitation to have children. Instead, I have been scared.

I had a traumatic experience with my first-ever pelvic exam right before Jordan and I got married. I've hesitated to apply the word "trauma" to myself, but the older I get, the more I can acknowledge that unpleasant, painful exam—for which I was completely unprepared, thank you, purity culture—set the tone for my future desires. At my Christian schools, I'd been told sex in marriage, especially if I waited to have it, would be mindboggling, a reward for years of self-control. And I was well into my twenties, maybe even my thirties, before I realized how much work getting pregnant could actually be. I'd reached the conclusion, based on abstinence-only sex education classes in middle and high school, pregnancies occurred all the time, with barely any thought or effort.

Not only did I have mental and emotional baggage regarding intimacy, doctors, and childbirth, but I didn't *feel* the things all my friends felt. I had friends who were desperate to become mothers; some felt passionately called to adoptive parenting, to fostering. No one I knew would ever use the word "ambivalent" to describe wanting children. The women I knew who wanted children faithfully tracked their fertility. They quit their stressful jobs. They planned their pregnancies and scheduled sex around ovulation and their husbands' work schedules. Meanwhile, I'd spent years working to teach myself sex could be fun. I wasn't about to create a recurring sex appointment with Jordan on my Google calendar.

For years, I kept waiting for the switch to flip, for motherhood to become the deepest desire of my heart. It never did, so I wondered if maybe motherhood wasn't meant for me.

It reminds me now of how I felt going wedding-dress shopping. I don't know where the mythology of wedding-dress shopping originated, but by the time Jordan and I were engaged, there were entire television programs devoted to finding the perfect dress. You'd sit and watch as brides and their mothers and friends traipsed into mirrored rooms together, drinking champagne, oohing and aahing, until, finally, the bride would stand on a pedestal in the center of the room and burst into tears over discovering just the right dress and veil.

When my mother and I embarked on my own wedding-dress shopping trip, we were confounded at every turn. So much tulle. So much lace. Fitting specialists would use jumper cable clamps to ensure the sample sizes fit correctly, and let me assure you: no one has ever picked out their perfect wedding dress looking like a Stegosaurus. One sales associate, when discovering I didn't want to wear a veil, informed me I'd be depriving my soon-to-be-husband of the best moment of his life. I turned and walked out of the store. I still hold a grudge against David's Bridal.

My point is I'd been sold the idea that I'd know which wedding dress was mine by my emotional response. I'd burst into tears, or get chills on my arms. My mother and maid of honor would look at me in awe. I would be transformed.

This did not prove true for me. I never cried, never got chills, even when my mother found a seamstress who made me a polka-dot wedding dress with short sleeves, and a short enough hem so I could wear my Converse tennis shoes. It was the perfect dress for me, but I didn't experience the hunt the way so many of my girlfriends did.

I see now I'd believed pregnancy and motherhood would function in the same way. I'd be ready for motherhood only if I was filled with a desperate need, if I'd move heaven and earth to have babies. I kept waiting for those feelings, and when they never came, I began to wonder if motherhood simply wasn't my life's calling.

In spiritual direction, my director will often ask me what I want. I hate this question. It feels selfish, even silly. I grew up doubting my own wants, not because my parents taught me to but because I was raised in a form of the Christian tradition where humans are not to be trusted. Our desires are fleeting, even flawed. To listen to what we want is narcissistic, self-indulgent, so when my director would ask me what I wanted, not only did I not know how to answer, but I thought it would be selfish if I did. When she gently showed me multiple places in Scripture where Jesus asks people what they want, I was shocked. I'd read the Bible repeatedly during my childhood, and somehow I'd forgotten this question is at the very heart of who God is. Which then made me realize what was also happening: If I articulated what I wanted, what would happen if the God I believed in didn't give it to me? Who would he be then? What would happen to my faith?

For years, my spiritual director and I worked on this question together. She and my therapist both wanted me to move beyond my ambivalence. They wanted me to know what I really wanted, even if motherhood played no role at all.

One March, prompted again by this question, I suddenly had an answer, a visceral one: "I want a loud house of belonging." I was stunned. My answer was a surprise to myself. It wasn't "I want a house and 2.5 kids," but in its own way, it was specific. I could see, in my mind's eye, this house, filled to the brim with joy. I couldn't see how many children were in the living room, but I could feel its warmth and hospitality. I finally could see what I wanted, and I didn't feel anxious or nervous or unresolved. I felt relieved. No matter what, I knew what I wanted, and I could articulate it.

I still have my notes from that direction session, scattered across the page. *Fear can be a friend. Jesus wants to muck around in your fear. God has so much capacity for love; she is maternal, inclusive, and expansive. Love is capable of expansion. My body is capable.*

My ambivalence was not caused by my career. I had legitimate anxieties and issues and fears—existential fears about identity (would I still be me if I became a mother?) and pragmatic fears about childbirth (could my narrow body handle a baby?). I also had preconceived ideas about feelings and emotions, ideas often compounded by societal expectations and norms. I misread what could have simply been healthy openhandedness as ambivalence or lack of desire.

I want a loud house of belonging, and that might mean a house full of kids, or—more likely, given my age—it might simply mean a house filled with people I love, however many of us there may be.

Life is not easy in the South for a woman over thirty-five without children. People have guessed I'm either career-driven, without time or capacity for children, or that I am barren and infertile. To my best understanding and knowledge, these assumptions are false. I have sat at breakfast tables and listened to unasked-for advice. I have been given gory details of people's birth stories. I have sat quietly during Mother's Day church services, choosing to focus on my gratitude for my own mother so I can ignore a well-meaning pastor's praise for life's "highest calling." I have been prayed over and anointed with oil. I have observed friends' miscarriages and worried about—then experienced—my own. I have been asked questions I hope you would not ask even your closest friend, and I have been asked them by near strangers. One afternoon, while I was working the register at the bookstore, a high school acquaintance I hadn't seen in years came in, and during the course of small talk, he asked if Jordan and I had kids. "Nope, not yet!" I said cheerfully, because that always seemed like the easiest and truest answer. He cocked his head. "You know how to make them, right?" And then he proceeded to encourage me to practice.

It can be hard to retain your dignity in the middle of all this.

I've never forgotten the phrase "loud house of belonging," now spoken three years ago; my spiritual director won't let me. I still do not look much like my peers. I am not desperately hopeful for children, though for a brief, eleven-week period, I was pregnant, and it felt like a miracle, and I was relieved and ecstatic and hopeful. I have not, thus far, undergone fertility treatments; I have only begun to pray for the family I think I long for.

My heart is broken for women I know, dear friends, who have wanted children since they were little girls themselves, who have crossed mountains for their children, women who have suffered multiple miscarriages or false alarms or medical treatments or traumatic births to bring their children into the world.

I have wondered what it means when your own suffering doesn't look exactly like that, when the waiting you've endured might not seem like suffering at all.

This is why I generally stay quiet at lunch tables and at baby showers, why I am mostly excited and rarely too envious when someone tells me they're pregnant. They deserve their hope. They knew what they wanted, and they did whatever it took to get it. Maybe what I'm really jealous of is that they figured it all out before I could or did.

Since clarifying my desire for a loud house of belonging, I have taken steps to make room. If Jordan and I do have children, is there room in our hearts? In our home? In my work? I have spent years continuing to identify and navigate my fears and anxieties. I have adjusted my work schedule at the bookstore, hiring staff and delegating responsibilities. I have done my very best to create a life that will be full, no matter what happens next, and I have tried to remember that my body is capable, that I am capable, and that love is expansive and inclusive.

I was thirty-five years old when I finally could articulate my hope to have children. I have been a late bloomer my whole life, but it is still lonely to find yourself in a different life stage from most of your peers. I have to constantly be okay with who I am and what I have chosen for myself. I still don't know what my loud house of belonging will look like. I don't know what steps Jordan and I will take next, or what parenthood might become for us. I remain cautious and hopeful, grateful for the full life we already live and already have. I love the Sondre Lerche lyric "Better be prepared to be surprised." That's how I want to live my life. Not dreading, not anxious, not exhausted, but prepared, perhaps, for a good surprise or two.

PART V

# Staying You

*Whether you think you know exactly who you'll become or you have absolutely no idea, I tell them, one thing is true for everyone, for better or for worse: Life will surprise you. You'll hit dead-ends and detours. There will be times when you can't fathom what comes next. When that happens, remember yourself as you are right now. Remember yourself as you were when you were even younger. Who were you when you weren't wondering who you were?*

—Mary Laura Philpott, *I Miss You When I Blink*

CHAPTER 20

# A Woman's Place Is in the Paint

M y mother, like so many boomer women before her, was, for
a time, obsessed with Oprah. I'd come home from school
on weekday afternoons, and at four, my mother—who, in my
memory, rarely sat still—would sit on the couch uninterrupted
for an hour to watch Oprah interview celebrities, talk about her
life and weight loss, and give guests free gifts they (and we) would
never forget.

It was during this season of Oprah-watching I remember my
mother talking a lot about "defining moments," the moments in
our lives we remember forever, the moments that cause us to pivot
or change or swing ourselves in a different direction. A defining
moment could be a divorce, a job loss, the loss of a parent or significant other. It could be positive, too: a graduation, a work success,
a life-changing comment from a teacher. My mother's "Oprah
moment" involved the flute.

My mom is the seventh of eight children, and all of them can play at least one instrument. My grandad played the piano and the guitar, and he had a beautiful singing voice I only vaguely remember, so rattled was it by emphysema in his later years. All of my aunts and uncles have lovely singing voices, my mother, too, and they played in their high school and college marching bands and sang in the choir and were generally a little reminiscent of the von Trapps.

In the sixth grade, it was my mom's turn to make it in the band. She desperately wanted to play the flute; her brothers all played the clarinet, and my mother wanted her own claim to fame. She recalls, vividly, all these decades later, being told by the band director her lips weren't right for the flute. She'd need, like her brothers before her, to play the clarinet.

She was devastated and refused. She never played an instrument, never joined the marching band, the only one of her siblings not to.

This is my mother's defining Oprah moment, and I heard about it whenever I experienced my own disappointments in middle school and beyond. That band director's words meant my mother's own children were strongly encouraged to play instruments. I took nearly a dozen years of piano lessons; Chet plays the guitar. Years later, when both of us had left home, my mom enrolled herself in guitar lessons, too. This teacher's one flippant comment about my mother's lips haunted her forever, maybe changed, in part, the trajectory of her life.

Because I grew up hearing my mother's Oprah moment identified and analyzed, I can, of course, name my own.

Throughout childhood, I played basketball: in little Saturday-morning leagues coached by my dad, in summer camps at our local colleges, in the driveway with my brother and our neighborhood friends. I loved basketball. I was ten years old when the Women's National Basketball Association launched, and I became obsessed with the New York Liberty and Rebecca Lobo, with Sheryl Swoopes (can you imagine a better name?) and Lisa Leslie and Cynthia Cooper. I loved them all, their beauty and their grace evident in every pass and dribble and layup.

I was a girl consumed. My favorite shoes were a child-size version of Grant Hill's FILAs. They looked ridiculous on my skinny, knock-kneed legs, but I loved them and proudly sported them with my pleated khaki shorts, a braided belt, a manatee necklace, and a T-shirt with an illustration of a WNBA basketball on the front proclaiming A Woman's Place Is in the Paint. I was twelve, and my favorite store in the mall was the Lady Foot Locker.

The summer before my seventh-grade year, I made the all-star team during our middle school summer camp. I was thrilled. I wasn't growing as fast as my peers, but I figured what I lacked in height I might make up for in speed. I was an extremely confident kid, and I wonder now if I was ever any good at basketball at all, or if I just had a convincing imagination. I believed I was destined for basketball greatness; thank God they finally had established a women's league. I'd have a career!

After the high of becoming a summer all-star, I was sure I was guaranteed a spot on my junior high basketball team. I realized I was leaving elementary school behind, so there were no sure things, but I knew the coach, and all my friends played, so I conditioned and applied myself at every after-school tryout. I recall really believing I'd make it. I was confident, but I also wasn't cocky, wasn't stupid. I knew I wasn't the best player, but I also knew I wasn't the worst. I worked hard, and I had a decent attitude. I figured if nothing else, I'd ride the bench and cheer my heart out for my friends on the court. The coach who'd put me on the all-star team was the coach of the junior high team, and I figured that was a good sign, too.

I don't know what school sports are like now; more competitive, is what I hear. But it felt pretty competitive back then, too, because the Monday after tryouts, the coach posted the new team roster in the gym, and I went with my friends, and I saw my name wasn't on the list.

It's become Annie lore, what happened next.

My friends' faces were filled with pity, and I think that's what I hated most, though I'm probably projecting, because that's definitely what I'd hate as the adult version of me. But back then, I was twelve, and all I distinctly remember is going to the coach's office and knocking on his door. I wanted him to tell me, to my face, why I hadn't made the team.

He did.

"You're too short and too skinny" were his exact words to me, further evidence I lived through the '90s. Girls' bodies were up for more debate back then. His words, even if true, stung, in part because he was a rather short guy himself, and in part because it meant skill had nothing to do with it. I couldn't change my genetics. I am a short person (five-two, though I definitely feel five-six) from short parents, but I'd thought, with practice, my height wouldn't matter. Of course, in basketball, height does matter, though my brother and I could name for you every short basketball player we'd ever heard of, including Spud Webb (five-seven) and Muggsy Bogues (five-three). And although it could be up for debate whether height matters in junior high sports, I'd asked for an answer, and I'd been given it. I nodded my head, thanked him for his time, and tried out for track a month or so later before breaking my toe and ending my athletic career forever.

I didn't want this to become my Oprah moment. I did not want to be defined by a coach's words to my seventh-grade self. But it *was* a pivotal moment, and it changed, at least partly, how I thought about myself. I still liked sports, still shot baskets on the hoop in our driveway, but I no longer dreamed about the WNBA. I turned my attention to academics, to writing, to wearing fake glasses and becoming the Barbara Walters of my generation. (I really loved Barbara Walters.) Still, though, in the deepest parts of myself resides a love of sports, basketball in particular.

The first summer of the pandemic, I was desperate to increase profit for a bookstore that remained closed to the general public. Like so many others, I'd found myself discombobulated as the pandemic continued, unable to focus on things I normally loved. My appreciation for literary fiction waned, and I found myself revisiting my favorite childhood books instead. My attention span was splintered, but even at peak pandemic, I could still lose myself in the words of Louisa May Alcott or Sharon Creech.

Enter The Baby-Sitters Club.

I don't know exactly why I wanted to revisit The Baby-Sitters Club during the pandemic. A new television adaptation was releasing on Netflix, and maybe I thought nostalgia would be comforting in a world falling apart. So Olivia, our shop manager, and Lucy, one of our staffers, joined me in reading The Baby-Sitters Club during the summer of 2020. We sold spots in a Baby-Sitters Back book club, mailed copies of the books all over the country, then Zoomed together every couple of weeks to discuss Kristy Thomas and the gang. My cousin designed '90s-inspired merch, and Lucy—a former musicologist from FSU—wrote us a theme song to the tune of the Backstreet Boys' "Backstreet's Back." I'm crying just thinking about it, because the idea was so simple and silly, a desire for a distraction in the middle of a global crisis, and it saved us. In the years since, I've met women from all over the country who found The Bookshelf during the pandemic, who read those *Baby-Sitters Club* books with us, who found a sliver of joy in a season void of it.

This is the power of our childhood obsessions.

That seventh-grade basketball coach didn't necessarily change my life with his well-meaning (if condescending) words. I was never going to play for the WNBA. Even at twelve, I bet in the back of my mind I knew that. But he temporarily robbed me of something I really loved, and I thought, wrongly, I had to find new things to love instead.

In high school, I threw myself into academics, joined the newspaper staff. I found new obsessions, and I'm grateful for them. They led me to future opportunities and set me on a career path. But in college, while I remained devoted to academic and journalistic pursuits, I tapped into my love of sports once again. I'd commandeer our dorm's common area to watch FSU football. I joined a social club (the Christian college version of a sorority) and played intramural sports, albeit not always well, though I did discover a passion for flag football. I cheered from the stands during basketball season, impressing my friends with an actual knowledge of the sport I'd loved as a kid.

When March Madness rolled around, I passed out brackets to friends and made bets with Jordan. We'd watch games together, and obsession once again reigned.

After college, that passion continued. Every March, Jordan dutifully sets up our family bracket competition through the ESPN app. We print our friends' brackets and tape them to the wall in our living room. The entire Bookshelf staff—none of whom I think has watched a game of basketball in their entire lives—participates in their own competition, and things get cutthroat and funny and creative, and it brings me so much happiness I can hardly stand it.

Now Jordan comes on the store podcast every March to talk about a book-inspired version of March Madness. It is, overwhelmingly, our most downloaded episode of the year, and I think it's because our banter is funny and Jordan is charming, but also because we are all so desperate for fun, for something that doesn't actually matter. The stakes are low, and the silliness is high, and it all reminds me of being eight and ten and twelve and wearing Grant Hill's tennis shoes with pride.

Maybe you, too, had a defining Oprah moment in childhood. Maybe you were told your lips weren't right for the flute, so you never picked up an instrument again.

Or maybe, like my mom, you did. You changed your story even after you thought there were expiration dates on what you could do. My mom started playing the guitar. I have a picture of her on my phone, in my aunt and uncle's living room, strumming away, doing something I think she never thought she'd do.

I don't play for the WNBA. I didn't become a coach or a manager or a sportswriter, either. Instead, every year, I lead my staff in our March Madness bracket competition. I remind them, gently, to have fun, to do something that doesn't matter, to try to participate in something they may never dominate. Every spring, Jordan breaks out every TV and computer we own, and we watch game after game after game, relishing in late nights and trash talk and squeaky tennis shoes on impossibly shiny floors.

Our childhood obsessions like basketball or The Baby-Sitters Club can save us. They can remind us of who we were before anything mattered, before everything felt heavy and hard. When life is overwhelming and challenging and our joy is stolen or hard to find, I think the things we once loved can bring us back, center us, make us whole. I watched a bunch of women survive the pandemic because of a book series about some spunky babysitters. I feel a little bit more like myself every March and April, when I stay up late watching a sport I've always loved.

Life is hard, but our innocent infatuations make it less so. That thing you loved in childhood? That sport or book series or TV show or board game? It can bring you back to yourself, if only for a moment, and a moment might be just what you need.

# CHAPTER 21

# Hair Is Everything

Before the global pandemic, before the "stolen election" cries of 2020, before January 6, before our worlds became more complicated and chaotic than we ever could have imagined, there was the perfect season of television that is *Fleabag*, season 2.

I did not watch *Fleabag* season 1. To some, this will be blasphemy, but I made it through only about half an episode before I blushed myself into a pile of ash, and my favorite pop-culture podcast assured me season 2 can stand on its own. So in the spring of 2019, I watched those six episodes over and over and over again, the way you might watch your favorite movie on repeat. At first, it was, of course, Hot Priest. The chemistry between Phoebe Waller-Bridge and Andrew Scott was palpable, filled with longing and depth, and I was mesmerized. It had been so long since I'd watched a good rom-com play out on screen. Their love story was complicated, verging on problematic, but I couldn't get enough.

The more I watched, though, the more my obsession became less about the show's romantic storyline and more about . . . everything else. I couldn't believe I was watching a television show that so accurately portrayed the dichotomy between faith and doubt, earnestness and cynicism. The writing was brilliant, the relationships intimate and human. And then there was the scene with the haircut.

Fleabag's sister, Claire—delightfully played by Sian Clifford—has gone to the hairdresser, armed, like so many of us on the days of our salon appointments, with a photo, only to come out looking, in her words, "like a pencil." Fleabag tries to assuage her concerns, assuring her "it looks French" (it doesn't, but these are the words all women long to hear), and together, the sisters march themselves back to the hairdresser for justice.

Justice doesn't come.

The haircut Claire has requested is exactly the haircut she has received; it simply doesn't look good *on her*. We, the audience, immediately see ourselves in Claire, in her desire to change her life with a pair of well-guided scissors. We've all been there, and when Fleabag defends her sister to the hairdresser with a rousing "Hair is everything!" speech, we jump up and cheer. (Or maybe that was just me on my living room couch.)

"Hair. Is. Everything," says Fleabag. "We wish it wasn't so we could actually think about something else occasionally. But it is. It's the difference between a good day and a bad day. We're meant to think that it is a symbol of power, a symbol of fertility, some people are exploited for it, and it pays your f*cking bills. Hair is everything, Anthony."

And we all know it is.

Women can track the exact stages and seasons of their lives based on their haircuts and styles. Don't believe me? I guarantee you can randomly encounter any episode of *Friends* and immediately deduce what season or year it's from by looking at Rachel's hair. Some of my friends are even known for their hair. Julie Anna has princess hair, long and luxurious, the stuff of fairy tales and the dream of hairdressers everywhere. My friend Courtney has had these blunt, cut-across bangs for as long as I can remember, and I knew the pandemic had gotten bad when she grew them out. Her face was still hers, of course, but I missed the bangs. I'd come to believe they were a part of her.

I have my own hair history, though you'd be hard-pressed to describe it, since I've had the same bobbed style since I was eight years old. The key to aging slowly, I think, is never changing your hair. A picture of me at eight could just as well be me at fifteen or me at twenty-five or me at thirty-two. I've tried a couple of deviations over the years, but they were outliers, even cries for help.

The summer I studied abroad in Italy, I got a perm just a few weeks before leaving. I don't even know if hairdressers will give you perms anymore, but I got one, not because I thought it would look good, but because—and this is true—I didn't want to haul a hair dryer to Europe. I figured my hair would air-dry best if it were curly, and since my hair already had a natural wave to it, a perm would give me just the body I needed to avoid a special European-plug adapter.

You know what? It looked cute. I looked nice with a perm.

Curly-haired women have always seemed low-maintenance, effortlessly fun, and for a summer, I joined their ranks. But then my hair grew, and I didn't maintain the perm's style, and as the school year progressed, I looked more and more like Hermione, the early years. No one told me how horrible it looked, which is a real testament to women's loyalty to one another. I'm grateful for the kid gloves, but I do look back and wish someone had told me to get a haircut, maybe a straightener.

Every spring, my university would host something called "Jamboree," a weekend's worth of musical performances produced by the school's social clubs. Each club would create and design a twenty-minute skit—complete with pop-music parodies and choreographed dance routines—then compete for that year's top prize. My wish for all of you is to experience something like Jamboree at least once in your lifetime, but you probably won't, so let me just say that there's no high like the "winning Jamboree" high. There's truly nothing like it.

My freshman year, the Jamboree theme was I Love the '80s, and our social club went fully meta, naming our skit "Video Killed the Reality Star." Our club's leadership soon realized I had nothing to offer in terms of rhythm or dance moves, so I was assigned one of the reality show characters, no dancing required. My role? Sharon Osbourne. I was instructed to wear all black and to dye my blunt bob a deep, dark red. Club leaders wanted me to cut my hair short and spiky, but I'm grateful even eighteen-year-old Annie knew that caliber of commitment was unnecessary.

I did, though, use temporary hair dye to achieve the requested color. My parents were appalled, and the color didn't wash out quite as fast as the packaging told me it would. That spring, my grandmother was diagnosed with cancer, and my entire family convened at my grandparents' home to rally and regroup. We took a picture with my grandmother by the fireplace mantel, and my awful red hair is front and center, cemented in our family's history, recorded for posterity.

There are other hair moments and memories, of course. The time I asked my mom's permission for highlights because my best friend had gotten them, only to chicken out because the decision felt too grown-up and permanent. (We put lemon juice in my hair that summer instead.) Or when Mary-Kate and Ashley popularized the zigzag part, and I insisted my mom recreate it for my ninth grade school picture. (I can't tell you how much I did not look like Mary-Kate or Ashley.)

My mom, it should be noted, does not recall these memories with the same detail I do. When I asked her if I'd ever gotten highlights in my teens, she texted back a million laughing emojis. The zigzag part? "I probably made you do that," she typed.

It is not in my nature nor in my reputation to care about these things. I was not an early adopter of fashion. I was not trendy or stylish. I didn't wear makeup until I was a junior in high school, and my mother did my mascara every morning until I went to college. I did not play with my looks, was not a child or teenager for whom dress-up was particularly fun or intriguing. I always, always wanted to look like myself.

The reason these distinct hair memories stick out so clearly for me is because they are anomalies in the relative evenness of my personality. I am not someone who changes how they look based on trends or popularity. I wear my hair as I have always worn it because it suits me, and I think if I did anything too drastically different, I would scare myself. I like recognizing the face I see in the mirror, but I also sometimes wonder: *Is it authenticity, or have I just been scared?*

I never got my nose pierced. (Text from my mother, verbatim: "Ear piercing was an ordeal, and honestly thrilled you did that!!!") I didn't dye my hair or go on a spring break trip and come back with culturally appropriated tiny braids (I see now: a blessing). I never got a tattoo. When I discovered my brother had, I was a little jealous. Why had I never done something like that? Was it really because I didn't want one? Was it because I thought it was wrong? Or was I simply being true to myself by refraining from what I might have perceived as excess displays of personality?

The perk of never changing your hair is never aging. As long as I keep this shoulder-length bob, I'll never not look like me, until— and this time is coming, I know—those same auburn tendrils begin to go gray, and I will have to decide: Which version of me am I most ready for? The one I once was, or the one I will be?

It's not that I regret never having highlights or getting a tattoo. I truly can't think of anything I like enough to permanently put it on my body. I don't regret those things. But I do wonder if my desire to stay comfortable has outweighed my desire to grow or to change. I wonder if my quest for consistency has robbed me of fun, of silliness, of playfulness. When a friend gets a tattoo or a piercing or bangs, I am in awe. I wish I could be so brave, less precious and particular with my body.

I wish these things because I know one day, I will change. If we're lucky, age comes for us all. My hair will go gray, and the wrinkles around my eyes will grow deeper. I might gain weight. If I am ever sick, I will lose that weight, and my skin will grow slack. When I see family pictures of my grandmothers on or near their deathbeds, I become emotional because they do not look like themselves. But they also don't look like they did when they were twenty or forty or even sixty.

Life changes us, even if we go to our hairdressers with the same inspiration photo, year after year after year.

I want to be more comfortable with the changes coming than I was in my youth. I want to occasionally wear lipstick or a shirt not in my usual color. I want to surprise myself, because one day I will look in the mirror and be surprised, and I want to be okay with that. I want to know underneath it all, I am still me, no matter the color or style of my hair.

# CHAPTER 22

# Sam Malone & a House with a Pool

I was perusing Zillow as one might have once perused the personals: not with any real interest or curiosity, but just for something to do. We had no intention of moving; we liked our small house on a street close to downtown. It had a porch—my only real criteria for our first home—and a swing and a backyard we could never seem to maintain. Our dog, Junie B., was buried there, beneath the often overgrown grass. Jordan had nearly given himself a hernia digging her burial plot, and I expected, perhaps naively, we'd live on Jefferson Street forever so as not to leave Junie behind.

But then I spotted a house on Zillow in our price range. It looked a little like an English cottage, plopped down in the middle of South Georgia, across the street from the park. You could, I thought, pretend you were living across from Central Park, maybe, with a little imagination.

And there, in the fenced-in backyard, was a pool.

I grew up in Florida. Pools felt normal, while simultaneously seeming like the stuff of wealthy people's homes. They were, according to my parents, high-maintenance, requiring a lot of attention and care. They were, according to statistics, unsafe, leading to accidental drownings and deaths. They were also fun.

We'd never had a pool at our house, but my aunt and uncle had an aboveground one for a few summers during my childhood. My brother, cousins, and I would make ourselves dizzy, swimming around and around the pool's perimeter, creating a whirlpool effect while reenacting the shipwrecks from *The Little Mermaid* or *Titanic.* Fun!

But when I saw the pool in the backyard of the house on Zillow, I thought: *Not for me. We can't have a pool. We won't take care of it. It adds too much expense.* A pool was beyond what I had pictured for myself. I felt, and I realize how this sounds now, not good enough for a pool. Not rich enough for a pool.

We went to look at the house anyway, for curiosity's sake. We still weren't in the market for a new home; we had no desire to move, but a slightly larger home in our price range only a few blocks from our current place was intriguing. Scheduling a viewing felt like what adults should do; it was our investigative duty.

One month later, we moved.

Here is what I like about living in a house with a pool.

I like wearing my bathing suit around the house. It's how other people must feel walking around naked or in their underwear, activities I personally do not enjoy. In my underwear, I feel exposed, on display. What if the UPS man comes to drop off a package? What if my blinds are open and the neighbors peer in? (Our blinds are always open.)

In my bathing suit, though, I feel like I am on vacation. I feel immediately relaxed. Getting a drink out of my refrigerator feels like taking a Coke down to the beach on a hot summer's day. I feel low-maintenance, calm. My metaphorical feathers become unruffled; I feel at ease.

Living in a house with a pool makes me think summer could be my favorite season. I take one look outside my kitchen window and think, *If I squint, it looks like I live by the ocean.*

During the spring and summer, my shoulders and nose become pink. Not in a "please put on sunscreen" way—I wear SPF 50 and live in constant fear of skin cancer—but in an I-am-young-and-healthy-and-fun way. My countenance screams: "I just spent all day outside instead of on the couch," even though I did not do any lawn work or hiking but instead read three books.

Living in a house with a pool makes me feel like the kind of woman I aspire to be. I am, by nature, a smidge addicted to work. I love multitasking and ambition and success. My identity tends to feel fully wrapped up in what I do.

With a pool, though, I feel more free. I check my phone less and stop and listen to the birds and the wind chime and the fountain. It is the same feeling I get when I'm on vacation, hundreds of miles away from work, only this is right outside my back door. I can leave the confines of my back hallway and step into a world in which my commitments are few, a world in which two pieces of

Lycra are acceptable coverings, and the smell of sunscreen drifts off my skin and onto the breeze.

A person with a pool is easygoing, laid-back.

So is a person with a dog.

When we got a dog, our world changed. I was less concerned with the state of my floors. I allowed crumbs and dog hair to coalesce, not in filth, necessarily, but in an unspoken admission that our house would never be fully and completely clean, because, after all, there was an animal living inside it.

Our friends found Junie B., an old beagle, wandering their neighborhood. They put posters up, knocked on doors, took her to the vet, but no one ever claimed her. Jordan and I had been looking for a dog with the zeal of two overthinking adults, and therefore hadn't found one. Junie B. became ours.

She never barked, had to be carried halfway through long walks, and always was willing to dress up for Halloween. She was the perfect pet.

And then she died, as pets are wont to do. She'd aged, and she stopped being able to move her hind legs, so one summer afternoon, we took one last family picture together, then drove her to the vet and had her put down. We stood by her side crying in the vet's room because we figured it was the least we could do for someone who'd been so loyal to us. It was one of the hardest and saddest things Jordan and I had done together, and I didn't think my heart would ever recover. I did not want another dog.

"One and done," I'd say, just like I do, still, about Jordan.

We left Junie buried in our backyard when we moved, and after a few years with a pool, I became laid-back enough to start thinking about another dog. We hadn't been able to have children, not yet, and the house was sometimes quieter than I like, even as someone who loves quiet. I missed Junie's company and kinship. It was time to try again. "Just no puppies!" I said.

So we scoured rescue websites and asked our friends and family members to keep an eye out for us. Once, I went far outside my comfort zone and attended a pet adoption event at a car dealership. I almost refused to get out of our own vehicle, but adulthood is realizing sometimes you're being a pill, so I got out with Jordan, and we met an older yellow lab named Dozier who seemed like the perfect fit.

We went on multiple playdates, and his foster mom brought him to the house for a home visit. It was such a contrast to Junie, who'd literally just walked into our lives, but good things, we believe, are worth time and effort, so we jumped through every hoop until the day Dozier came home to live with us.

It was, in a word, horrific.

Over the course of the weekend, we were prisoners in our own home, playing classical music for anxious dogs from a YouTube channel we'd found. Jordan left trails of cheese to try to gently coax Dozier out of our dining room, where he'd refused to eat or go to the bathroom for thirty-six hours. He became territorial and aggressive, baring his teeth, his hair standing on end.

I was no longer easygoing. This was not fun, for him or for us.

We called his foster mom, who was apologetic. Aggression wasn't his usual MO, but he'd become attached to her. Something was wrong, so she picked him up, and we once again were dogless. Childless.

But we had a pool, and I kept searching rescue websites. The bookstore's manager bought a goldendoodle puppy, and I thought: *Maybe we could do a puppy after all?* But I didn't feel like a puppy person. I didn't think I was patient enough or nurturing enough. Puppies were for dog people, and I wasn't really a dog person, just a Junie person.

Then my mom found a litter of English retriever puppies on Facebook. She sent us photos, and they were, as you'd expect, adorable. I don't have a complete heart of stone. Jordan suggested we go see them in person, and they were equally adorable there, but I still wasn't convinced. We had a summer of travel ahead. It would be irresponsible to bring a puppy home. We were not puppy people.

Jordan Jones rarely asks for things. He never issues ultimatums or makes executive decisions in our marriage. We're a team, and we play like one. But on the drive home from visiting those puppies, he came the closest he's ever come to begging. I laid out my hesitations, and Jordan issued responses for each.

Two weeks later, we brought home our new puppy, Sam Malone. He is lying at my feet as I write this book, a thing I wanted to be true and now somehow really is.

I don't know why I didn't think I was good enough or wealthy enough to have a pool. I don't know why I didn't think I was nurturing enough or capable enough to train and raise a puppy. Those beliefs I had about myself weren't true. I know myself well, but in those cases, I was wrong.

A pool and a puppy have been two of the best things to happen to me over the last few years.

Our home is now filled with Sam's blond, wispy hair. My clothes are covered in it, too. I swore a dog would never be allowed on our bed, but each morning when Jordan leaves for work, Sam jumps up into ours, keeping me company, resting a paw on my leg until my alarm goes off. There are dirty paw prints on our floors, and in the summer, our back hallway is filled with wet towels and drippy bathing suits.

A puppy made me breathe a little easier, made me take all the attention off myself and my ambition. A pool in the backyard makes me carefree in the same sort of way. I like who I am without makeup, with my hair tucked under a baseball cap. I like a slight gleam of sweat on my chest, the Tervis Tumbler filled with lemonade, the stack of books on the Adirondack chair. I like slipping on my fake Birkenstocks from Target, looking in the mirror, and thinking: *That is the face of a chill person.*

I long, in the deepest parts of myself, to be calm, to be relaxed, and a pool helps. So does Sam. With a pool in my backyard, it's not that I feel like a different person. It's like I'm the person I was always meant to be. Sun-kissed, unburdened, carefree.

With Sam, I am funny and comfortable and at home. He noses my phone out of my hand and wags his tail with joy when I walk in from work. He comes to the bookstore and looks out the upstairs window, and he doesn't know I sometimes don't belong. I belong to him. He belongs to me. That's enough. That's the only knowledge he needs.

Not everyone should have a pool in their backyard, nor should everyone get a puppy. (I don't think.) But I do think we should stop limiting ourselves to the things we assume we might deserve or want or need, because what if we need something else? What if we miss out on something truly lovely because we think we'd hate to be surprised?

I am, in my life, concerned with a congruity of personality. I value authenticity, and I loathe change. I like being consistent. I like the idea that if someone encounters me on Instagram, then meets me in person, they will discover I am one and the same. I like knowing you'd recognize me anywhere, whether I was twelve or twenty-three or thirty-six. I am the opposite of a surprise. I like it that way.

But I worry, too, that my obsession with my own consistency means I have missed out on things like pools and puppies, things I waved off as being "not for me." As it turns out, pools and puppies are very much *for me*. In fact, maybe I need them to help me step out of my norms, to awaken myself to the beautiful possibilities that exist when we let go a little bit, when we allow ourselves to try something new on for size.

I love having a pool. I love swimming laps and feeling like a little girl again. I love reading there, with Sam stretched out near my lap. I love that we got a puppy. I love that we have known Sam for his whole life, and that we are all he will ever know. I loved his squirmy, fluffy, tiny body, how I could hold him in one hand. And now I love that he pulls me around on walks and forces me out of my head and smiles at me when he suspects I've had a bad day.

I am glad I let myself be surprised by these things. I hope more surprises are coming. Life is better with a little bewilderment and wonder about the things we think we might not deserve.

# CHAPTER 23

# A Life Lived with Books

When I was eight years old, I hid in the closet to cry over *Little Women*. I could not get over Laurie's betrayal of Jo, could not believe he married Amy, who'd burned Jo's book in a fit of jealousy. It was the first time I remember a book making me feel something. I'd loved books before—American Girl books, Nancy Drew, The Boxcar Children—but I'd never been moved to tears over one, and I hid in the closet so I could cry in private.

I've returned to *Little Women* many times over the years, trying to see if Jo still resonates as deeply with me in adulthood as she did when I was a young girl with writerly aspirations of her own. I see so much of myself in Jo, still. Yes, because she is a writer. Yes, because her closest friend and confidant is a boy. Yes, because she is fiercely loyal. But mostly yes, because she doesn't want to grow up. She doesn't want things to change. She's most emotional, most grieved, over the loss of her sisters to adulthood. I have long been the same, clinging desperately to a younger version of myself, to the nostalgia of a life lived before.

I wonder if this is why I love books. I can dip my toe into other lives without entirely changing my own. I can stay, because in books, I can adventure and wander, meander and dream.

One of the questions most often asked of me as a bookseller and bookstore owner is whether reading is still fun. "Has it become work?" I'll get asked by a stranger or podcast listener or friend.

The most honest answer is yes and no. Yes, reading occasionally feels like work to me. There are assignments and deadlines and required page counts. But it is the most fun work I have ever done, and reading is still very much a treasured pastime for me. If my husband and my family and my faith all ground me, reading a good book cements that grounding. I feel most myself around the people who love and know me best, and books are among my dearest friends and cohorts.

In a bizarre turn of events no one in my life could have predicted, much of my days are spent in a public-facing capacity. I am, somehow, a podcast host, an Instagram personality (please, God, no), and a bookstore owner whose best days are spent interacting with the community she calls home. In every personality quiz I have ever taken, I am soundly an introvert, and when I tell people this, they balk. They cannot believe it. This is because they do not see what I look like when I arrive home from my days.

After one particularly busy, event-filled week at the bookstore, I once told a newish staffer in passing I felt like a "shell of a person." Longtime booksellers were used to me dropping this line (it's a phrase I use often, in competition with "Do you ever feel like a plastic bag?" and "I'm going to collapse in on myself like a dying star"), but this woman was horrified. "Are you okay?" she asked, genuinely concerned for my well-being. I was stunned by her response. Did she not feel like a shell of herself after a week like that? Reader, she was an extrovert, so she did not.

I come home each afternoon and engage in something Jordan lovingly calls "Annie time." Because Jordan commutes from Tallahassee each day, I arrive home much earlier than he does, particularly now that my schedule is a little more flexible than it used to be. "Annie time" is really just "quiet time." I take Sam for a walk while listening to an audiobook. I take a nap on my couch. I watch a TV show I like. And on my best days, I curl up in our little reading room and get lost in the world of words.

It's okay, I think, to feel like a shell of a person, a shell of myself. I give a lot to my job, to the people around me, to the people I love. The key is refilling my tank, reembodying my depleted self. The way for me to do this best is in my home, armed with a cozy chair and a good book.

Over the years, I have gotten lost in thrillers set on hijacked airplanes; become an honorary daughter to large, dysfunctional families with memorable matriarchs; rolled my eyes at countless East Coast blue bloods and badly behaving rich people; fallen in love with rom-coms Nora Ephron would envy or at least appreciate. I have revisited the classics of my childhood, including *Little Women*, but also *Bloomability* and *The Baby-Sitters Club*, *Emily of New Moon*, and the works of Joan Bauer. I have discovered a love of poetry (thank you, Kate Baer) and encountered modern American novelists who I believe deserve a place in the canon (Jesmyn Ward, Lauren Groff). I've felt seen in the essays of Mary Laura Philpott and Shauna Niequist and Beth Ann Fennelly. I've laughed at David Sedaris and R. Eric Thomas and cried over Marilynne Robinson and Elizabeth Strout. I've left my reading chair agog and hungover from prose I wish I could call my own.

Books fill me up. Quiet fills me up. My home fills me up.

I read books because, yes, by some twist of fate and act of serendipity, it is my job. I read books because, at their best, they make me better, more empathetic, more socially aware, more in tune to the stranger beside me. They help me imagine a better future, provide answers to my insatiable questions, take me to places I'll never get to go. I read books because they are an easy point of entry to relationship. They spark conversations and make me an enjoyable dinner companion (I hope). Books eliminate my awkwardness, awaken my expertise, and move me forward when I want to stay put. I read books because they fill up my depleted soul and give me renewed energy for a life spent outside the walls of my home and the safe pages of the novels I love.

Books aren't meant to be hiding places, defenses against a dark world, excuses for detachment and disengagement. I think they're meant to be flashlights, moving us forward, placing us in community with one another, giving us a reason to walk together.

I have disappeared into books since I was a young girl, and I love disappearing into them today. I love leaving this world for a couple of hours and immersing myself in another one. But I also love turning a page and closing a cover, because I know now I have the renewed energy to exit the contours of my chair and become, once again, a wife, a daughter, a boss, a friend, a person.

Books, by some paradox, help me engage more fully in the world around me.

This is why I read, why I see myself and my friends in the characters authors have created and in the worlds they have built for us. I read to live more solidly in this world, curl up in quilts and sit by open windows or outside by the pool, always with a book because it brings me comfort and cures my loneliness and assuages my fears.

Books bring me back to myself.

A few years into our marriage, Jordan and I became obsessed with *Up*, a British documentary series following fourteen children from 1964 until present, with a new, updated film releasing every seven years. The first film debuted when the children were seven; they're now well into their sixties, and the series follows them through the ups and downs of college, marriage, divorce, middle age, children, and grandchildren.

Each film opens with footage from the original 1964 installment; the children are young and vivacious and giggling, and they play together as the narrator lays out the film's premise: "Give me a child until he is seven, and I will show you the man."

It's a Jesuit motto (sometimes also attributed to Aristotle), but the film uses it to suggest that who these children are at seven will undoubtedly determine who they are in adulthood. And although the children grow and change over the years, the motto seems to ring eerily true: who they were at seven is, at least in part, who they are at twenty-one, thirty-five, forty-nine, fifty-six, sixty-three.

I still think about this show every so often, though it's been years since I've seen one of the episodes. I google the participants, but I also think about the simplicity of the concept. I look back on my parents' footage of me as a child, and I wonder if when I was seven, I could have predicted who I would become.

At seven, I was quiet. I adored school. I wanted to be a teacher like my aunt and a writer like my grandfather. I loved my family and treasured my friends, but I was perfectly content playing alone or reading a good book.

A love of books is the through line of my life, a hobby I can trace back to my earliest childhood memories and immediately weave through my middle school and high school selves, right into my choice of university and the selection of my spouse. I wanted to be a writer because of books, and when the opportunity came to own a bookstore, that love of books played a huge role in my scared-but-brave yes.

On my lonely days or my hard days or the days when I feel least like myself, I try to pick up a book. At this point, it's partly reflex, a habit long ago instilled. But mostly just holding a book reminds me of the less-burdened childhood version of me. When I pull a book out of my bag or off my shelf, when I visit a bookstore or a library, when I stay up late for just one more chapter, I'm no longer Annie the bookstore owner. I'm not Annie the boss, not Annie the wife, not even Annie the friend. I'm Annie the reader, the title I've held longest and perhaps most proudly. She is who I was at seven and who I am now.

I'm thrilled and relieved whenever I see her, so grateful for a friendly face.

# CHAPTER 24

# The Importance of Being Earnest

I had known and dated Jordan for nearly four years before our families met one another. It was his graduation weekend, and we ate lunch at a barbecue restaurant, and Jordan's somewhat stately grandfather crossed his arms over his chest, leaned back, and pronounced: "I see now that Annie has the enthusiasm of her mother and the sobriety of her father." It makes me laugh every time I think about it, not because it's inaccurate, but because of how eerily spot-on the assessment was and continues to be.

Over the years, I've seen plenty of sobriety out of my mother and enthusiasm out of my father—long-term partners can't help but morph a bit into each other—but Jordan's granddad made a remarkably astute comment that day, in a few moments boiling down my family to the roles we've inhabited and the traits we've carried for years.

It's true: I am a highly introverted but enthusiastic person.

("Annie's quiet, not shy," my first-grade teacher told my mother.) One look at my face will tell you exactly what I am thinking; you will never wonder where I stand, even if I'd like for you to be in the dark just a moment longer. I once sat around a table for a group discussion in college, attempting to be inconspicuous, only to have the professor call on me because he "could see I had something I wanted to say." Those words haunt me at every board meeting I attend, so it took me a long time to see this personality quirk as anything remotely akin to strength.

A few years ago, I purchased tickets for me and my cousin Ashley to attend a fall weekend along Massachusetts's North Shore. My friend Melissa was hosting a girls' weekend built around leaf-peeping and a tour of Orchard House, Louisa May Alcott's home in Concord. I'd been there once, in my early twenties, and since *Little Women* sits near the top of my favorite-books-of-all-time list, I felt a return visit was in order. Ashley and I flew to Boston; I miraculously navigated the highways, and we found ourselves surrounded by the most glorious yellows and reds and browns you can possibly imagine. It was unlike any southern fall I'd ever experienced, and I couldn't believe I was lucky enough to be there.

As we traipsed through the oldest working farm in America, surrounded by dancing, glittering leaves, I wanted to stop and cry. It was so beautiful, and at one point, when we found ourselves standing with the rest of our tour group in front of the home of author Margaret Sidney (*Five Little Peppers and How They Grew*), Melissa looked over at me. "Look at Annie's face!" she said to the group, and I didn't know why, except it turns out the awe I was experiencing on the inside I was apparently showing on the outside: big eyes, mouth agape, verging on tears. Ordinarily, I might have been embarrassed by the attention, but as someone who works in customer service and hosts parties and events, I now know all you really ever want is for one person to look like they love what you've created.

And I did. I loved the trip Melissa and her friends had so meticulously planned, loved experiencing a New England fall, loved every attention to detail, every antique store, every lobster roll.

When was the last time you loved something, and it showed?

For years, there has been no shortage of discussion about our age of cynicism, how we rage and critique and criticize because it is popular and seemingly intelligent, even cool (though adulthood is supposed to cure us of the desire to be cool).

I'm not sure, though, there's been enough discussion on the solution, on the antidote. I've read articles titled things like "Love What You Love" and "To Be Cringe Is to Be Free," and those are good places to start. Really, though, I want to live in a world where we love what we love, and we aren't afraid to show it: on our faces, in our words, with our actions.

In 2019, The Bookshelf began hosting Reader Retreats. I've long had an apprehension for summer camps—don't they feel culty to you?—but I thought maybe, if there could be an introverted, bookish version, that could be fun. So our staff developed a weekend's worth of readerly events and began hosting women from all over the country at our store and in our town. Year after year, our staff ranks our retreats as their favorite part of Bookshelf life and work, even though it takes weeks and months of preparation and recovery time.

We've hosted almost a dozen retreats at this point, which means, even if you account for repeat attendees, we've probably entertained nearly two hundred women over the years, and you know who my favorite ones are? They're not the retreaters who read the most or ask the most thoughtful questions or buy the most books. (Though trust me, I appreciate every single one of those types of retreaters.) My very favorites are the ones who I can tell are having a great time. The women who aren't afraid to laugh heartily or grin giddily, the ones who take photos and express gratitude and pull staffers aside to share their awe.

The solution to an age of disenchantment? Be enchanted. Share about it.

I used to think my face betrayed me, like it told secrets I wasn't ready to share.

But now I don't want my awe to be tucked inside, away from the very people who might need it most. Awe begets awe, enchantment begets enchantment.

In a world of cynicism, earnestness is crucial.

I want to be the kind of person whose mouth sits open at a sunset, who notices a new rosebush planted in a neighbor's yard. I don't want to be known for my eye roll but for my awe. Life and its pleasures are so fleeting, so I want to love and lean into the wonders we often take for granted: spring baseball games and the smell of burgers on a grill. Sprinkler water and dancing yellow leaves and

THE IMPORTANCE OF BEING EARNEST

waves crashing on the shore. Puppy dog breath and baby giggles and good books that end with just the right sentence.

Of all the people I follow or encounter or befriend, my favorites—the ones I'm drawn to without hesitation—chase awe and share it. Love what you love, yes, but also don't keep it to yourself.

Last year, in the middle of the March Madness season, our bookstore team created merchandise revolving around books and basketball and a nun named Sister Jean.

Sister Jean is a 104-year-old chaplain at Loyola University, serving and ministering to the men's basketball team. She became "internet famous" back in 2018 when the Loyola Ramblers unexpectedly went to the Sweet Sixteen. I loved her the moment I laid eyes on her, and I shared that love with the Bookshelf staff. Soon, we all became enamored with Sister Jean, and when it came time to celebrate March Madness and design accompanying store merchandise, we decided Sister Jean needed her own T-shirt.

Once we'd had the design printed, Jordan, in his Enneagram 3 wisdom, told me I should send Sister Jean one, so I did. A few weeks went by, and I wondered if the shirt had ever found its way into Sister Jean's hands. Then, in the middle of a manager meeting one morning, one of our staffers knocked on my office door, then poked her head in. "Sister Jean is on the phone for you!" she exclaimed excitedly.

I wish I had a video of that moment, because I leaped out of my chair and scrambled for the phone, hands immediately sweaty, heart pounding, and tears in my eyes. Sure enough, Sister Jean was on the phone.

The Bookshelf staff watched as I talked to her, for maybe five or six or seven minutes—I can't be sure, because I entered some kind of fugue state. Sister Jean, in all her calm and quiet wisdom, was talking to me on the phone.

Much of what she said I want to remain preserved in only my memory, but I will share this: she spoke about how much she loved the shirt, and how she'd looked up the bookstore and could tell I loved what I did. "I tell my students all the time," she said, "find a job you love, because if you don't love it, you'll make everyone else around you miserable."

It's so different from the "Love what you do, and you'll never work a day in your life" mentality, which I've found over the years to be, at best, trite, and at worst, deceitful. It's something I've discovered to be utterly untrue.

But "Love what you do, because if you don't, you'll make everyone around you miserable"? Well. That's something that sticks, something that's true.

When I hung up the phone that day with tears in my eyes, here is what I looked around and saw: three women, who ten years ago had probably never heard of Sister Jean or watched a college basketball game, all smiling widely, laughing, maybe even tearing up with me. They loved what I love. They weren't afraid to express their enthusiasm or excitement or appreciation. Keila made me a commemorative sign for my office door. Olivia, Erin, and Kyndall took videos and photos. We had a collective moment of awe, and although Sister Jean's phone call was the spark, the staff's excitement was the flame.

It reminds me, a little, of this wonderful G. K. Chesterton quote about how God inexplicably and patiently causes the sun to rise every day, how he delights in redundancy and monotony in a way it seems only children can.

Every time I see a live theater performance, I think of that quote. Of how actors and performers give us this beautiful gift of doing the same thing, night after night, over and over, in excellence and with joy, all so we can feel as if they're doing it for the very first time. They give us the gift of magic, and it's why I cry at the end of nearly every play I've ever seen. It's because I've witnessed something holy. I've witnessed a group of people who love what they do, then turn around and share it with the world.

Love what you love, and let other people see it, so they can love it, too.

Love your books and your musicians and your fan fiction and your TV characters and your poetry and your backyard and the fresh strawberry you picked right off the vine. Love it and share it with me. I want to love it all, too.

## New York or Nowhere

I have a beanie I bought in New York. I live in South Georgia, so my opportunities to wear beanies are few and far between, but I adore winter wear, and hats are no exception. So I bought this beanie as a souvenir, and I wear it a few days out of the year. It's teal, and on the front, embroidered in white, are the words *New York or Nowhere*.

When I was seventeen, the summer before my senior year of high school, I visited New York City for the first time. I'd just broken up with my high school boyfriend (a term I hesitate to use as it never feels fully accurate—so brief, so innocent, so lacking in romance), and my aunts and uncle took me on the trip as an early graduation present. I'd been desperate to go for years, because, like so many millennials before me, I'd been raised on sitcoms and rom-coms set in New York: *Friends, When Harry Met Sally, You've Got Mail, How to Lose a Guy in 10 Days, Serendipity, Two Weeks*

*Notice,* even *Sleepless in Seattle,* though its title suggests otherwise. Every female journalist I knew—and by "knew," I mean "encountered in books or television or movies"—moved to New York so their lives could begin. It's where I wanted my life to begin, too.

So I went with my family, and we toured the Statue of Liberty and found the port on Ellis Island where my ancestors entered the country so many years ago. We didn't eat at great restaurants or see Tony Award–winning shows, but I bought a key chain from Bloomingdale's so I could have one of their famous brown bags, and there's a picture of me with my lanky arms spread wide, grinning from ear to ear in Times Square. It was everything I'd dreamed. Not a single disappointment from that trip resides in my memory.

I went back to New York, this time with a friend, right before getting married. We flew into the city on separate flights, and I'd never felt so adult. We rented a hotel room in the Financial District, probably because it was cheaper, and we walked everywhere, through borough after borough after borough. We were late to the off-Broadway show we'd gotten lottery tickets for, and we took the wrong subway train one night, rescued near midnight by a cab driver who never made us pay out of concern for our safety. It was no longer the city of my dreams—I was aware, I think, I'd already forfeited that dream through my life's choices—but somehow it still lit me up inside.

One winter, for our anniversary, Jordan and I rode the train into Penn Station and took a Nora Ephron–inspired tour of the Upper West Side. (It wasn't an official tour, just me with cell phone in hand, googling the set addresses of all those movies I loved.) One summer a few years later, The Bookshelf paid for me to attend the now-defunct BookExpo; Jordan and I splurged on tickets to *Hamilton* and ran into some podcast listeners from Georgia while waiting in line. It felt ridiculously serendipitous, like the kind of thing that can happen only in New York. We got caught in a torrential rainstorm, which should have been inconvenient, but instead—perhaps due to my own naivete regarding city living— was incredibly humorous, even romantic. I loved how equalizing the rain was, everyone around us sopping wet, drenched and unattractive, umbrellas rendered useless. I loved it.

After talking about it for years, I finally took my cousin Ashley for her first-ever city visit, and we landed in New York at 4 a.m. in the middle of a blizzard. So much snow blanketed Central Park that we giggled and took picture after picture, FaceTiming our families back home in disbelief and awe. We sat in the Winter Garden Theatre and witnessed the incomparable talent of Sutton Foster and Hugh Jackman, live and in person. The whole time I felt utterly transported. I loved showing my cousin the city, as if it were a gift I could bestow upon her, despite it not really being mine to give.

These are the memories New York holds for me, and the seventeen-year-old version of myself who wondered if that New York trip was a once-in-a-lifetime experience can rest easy knowing I've found my way back there, time and again.

Of course, I've never lived there.

My love for the city feels like the closest I will ever come to having an affair. I am entirely satisfied with my life—my rooted, southern, stay-in-one-place life—but I am also intrigued by a city with public transportation and restaurants open past 9 p.m. I long for the anonymity, for the proximity of strangers, for the walkability, for the hustle and bustle. On every visit we've made together, Jordan comments how New York energizes me. Our first time there, he kept looking at me in wonder, like he didn't know I could be so soothed by a landscape utterly unlike our own.

Over the last few years, I've encountered friends and internet acquaintances and podcast personalities and authors who, after years of dreaming and planning, have now chosen to call New York home. They've entirely or partially uprooted their lives to accommodate the plans of their childhoods or early adulthoods, only now they're in their forties, their fifties, and their midlife adventures give me hope for my own one day.

But in the back of my mind is that niggling jealousy I first encountered most deeply in my twenties, as I watched my friends move and leave. Somehow, all these years later, I am still here. I haven't moved. I haven't left.

I still own a bookstore in a small town, still run the podcast I started more than a decade ago. I still don't have children. Jordan still works across the state line, and we still live miles and miles away from a major US airport. It takes us a minimum of two flights to go almost anywhere. I still live up the road from my parents. I still, somehow, call the South home. I am constantly in wonder and at odds with its beauty and brutality. Our door still swells shut every summer, and even though August makes me question everything, the truth is, I don't hate any of this. This is just what it's like to live here, to be home, to stay.

Maybe one day, Jordan and I will live in New York part-time. Maybe I will love it just like I always thought I would. Or maybe not. I may never know.

What I do know is for now, I stay. And the stories I live here are as consequential, as interesting, as dynamic as anything I could have encountered in a larger city, even in the greatest city in the world.

The people I love are living their stories, too, in cities scattered all over the map.

I wanted to write a book for people who stayed, but I also wanted to honor those who left. Because eventually, we'll all do a lot of both, leaving and staying. Even us stayers will one day be dust. We'll leave, too, and I hope we will have learned how from those who went first.

When people I love leave their families, their churches, their institutions, their towns, their neighborhoods, their cities, I want to wish them well. I want to be able to hold their leaving and honor it. I want to pay attention to their whys. I want them to know I'll be here waiting if they ever want to return.

There's a song I love by singer-songwriter Noah Kahan. (I feel, sometimes, like I'm just outside Kahan's average age demographic, but I'm pleased to report it doesn't matter. I went to his concert in Tallahassee and was one of the oldest people in the room. It didn't stop me from dancing and singing and generally being filled with joy.) In "You're Gonna Go Far," he alludes to the tension so many of us hold when the people we love choose or need to go. How he holds that tension is how I want to hold it, too. Kahan writes about life being hard where he is and that he's glad the person he loves is far away from the mess he has stayed behind to clean up. He encourages his friend to pack up his car, and he wants him to know: He's not angry. It's okay to leave. And it's okay to stay.

I do not live in New York. Not Chicago or Dallas or Boulder or Nashville or Kansas City or even Atlanta or Chattanooga or Savannah or Birmingham. But I know people who do. Their stories are good, too. The people I love who have left have inspired me in their leaving. They make me know leaving is possible. Sometimes it is even preferable.

When I have had to leave—my church, my hometown, my unhealthy relationships—I have channeled their strength, their spirit of tenacity and energy.

But I know staying requires strength, too. There's a line in Kahan's song about "good land," this idea that taking care of the places we've been given requires serious stamina. I think it's curious the listener can never tell from the lyrics: Does it require more strength to leave, or to stay?

Both, is my guess.

Where I am is good land. It is rich with stories to be mined and ordinary adventures to live. It takes, as Kahan sings, a strong hand and a strong mind.

I bet your life requires those things too, wherever you are.

My New York beanie is a fun souvenir. I love it, and I wear

it proudly, and I also don't entirely believe it. *New York or No-where*? No.

Good stories are anywhere you are. Your quiet, ordinary life matters, and the place you're living it matters, too.

We can't all move to New York. We can't all leave; some of us, for whatever reason or purpose, have to stay.

We'll keep the porch light on.

# Acknowledgments

I have always adored the acknowledgments section of a book, I have long loved getting a glimpse into the psyche of a writer, seeing a list of who or what makes them tick. The acknowledgements exist as a poignant reminder that the most solo-seeming projects cannot be completed or even attempted alone.

Here, then, are mine.

Thank you to Emily P. Freeman, who helped me realize my "next right thing" was to write the book proposal that ultimately became *Ordinary Time*. Jamie Tarence, thank you for generously introducing me to the right people and making connections when I didn't know how. Jonathan Merritt, thank you for seeing something in my writing you believed other people might want to read; you have been just the advocate and midwife I needed. To Angela Guzman and the team at HarperOne: there aren't words to express my gratitude to you for taking my Google Doc and turning it into a book I get to sell in my bookstore (and see in other bookstores, too). For a girl with a box of journals under her bed, this is a dream come true.

To the teachers who shaped and transformed my life: Mrs. Burgess, Dr. Walker, and Mary Ellen Cheatham. I think about you all the time. This book is partly yours.

Hunter Mclendon, outside of my family, you're the first person to read this manuscript in its entirety. Your enthusiastic, joy-filled response to this book's publication is something I will never forget. I hope I am half the writer and friend you are.

I never knew I could have so many friends. Morgan and Rachel, you have known me longest, and to be able to include you on this list and in this book is an honor. Being loved and known by you keeps me rooted and grounded in a way I desperately need. Julianne, Jenn, and Mandy: Thank you for holding tight to our friendship across time zones and life changes. You have never stopped cheering for me. The women in my mastermind group and on that life-changing trip to London have helped me feel less alone in creativity and entrepreneurship; putting words to a page felt attainable because of your encouragement. To the Swains (all of them: Jordan, David, Sherly—who specifically asked for her name to be in the acknowledgements—and Evia), you are our most kindred of spirits. Thank you for walking every road with us. Thank you to Hallie, who read my blog and knew I could write a book and told me so, and to Erin: our long walks make Thomasville feel more like home.

In adulthood, I have surrounded myself with people who are

ACKNOWLEDGMENTS

smarter than me and help me stay steady. Julie and Randi, "thank you" hardly feels adequate. Michelle, I could write because you cleared my calendar and helped me say no. Thank you.

To Thomasville, my adopted town: I'm not sure either of us got quite what we bargained for, but I am honored to call you mine. To every Bookshelf staffer past and present, but especially to Olivia, Erin, Nancy, Caroline, Kyndall, Keila, Esme, Lucy, Kate, Mallory, and Laura, you have lived so much of this story with me, and the work of your hands made my own achievable. Working alongside one another is one of the best parts of my life. And to indie bookstores everywhere and the people who work in them: I am so glad you exist in this world. Your communities are better because of the magic you offer.

Published books don't become a reality without readers, and in the last decade, readers have changed my life over and over again. Thank you to The Bookshelf customers and podcast listeners who believe in our store and its mission, and in me, by extension. You make my job one worth doing, and I love what I do because of you. I hope this book makes that clear.

For the Joneses: It's hard to have a writer in the family. Thank you for letting me in and for being excited and proud of the work I do.

My life was woven and spun out of an extended family filled to the brim with writers and storytellers, far too many to name here. But Lisa and Ray, thank you for being there for every single one of my life's milestones. Your love isn't lost on me. To my fuzz-ins whom I adore, Ashley and Caroline, thank you for loving the goofiest parts of me and for granting me honorary status as your big sister. Aunt Neena: You believed I could, so I did. Thank you.

For Mom, Dad, and Chet: I always wanted to write your names in my book, and now I did. Being raised by you and with you has made me the luckiest. I am so glad to be your daughter and sister. Thanks for letting me share you with the world (or with whoever reads this book). I love you.

Jordan, when we met, you said to me in passing, "When you write your book." Not if, but when. You knew. Your belief in me has held me up. Thank you for loving me well and for being my friend. Our marriage means more to me than I ever could have imagined, more than any words I could ever write.

This book and its stories have been swimming around in my head for longer than I care to admit. Now, dear reader, they're yours. I hope you see your life is a story, too.

## About the Author

Annie B. Jones is a writer, podcaster, and the owner of The Book-shelf, an independent bookstore in Thomasville, Georgia. She hosts *From the Front Porch*, a weekly podcast about books, small business, and life in the South, and her work has been featured in *Southern Living* magazine. A native of Tallahassee, Florida, Annie lives in Thomasville with her husband, Jordan, and their dog, Sam Malone.